PROGRESSIVE

BEGINNER

HARMONICA

by

Peter Gelling

The Progressive Series of Music Instruction Books, CDs, and DVDs

Visit our Website
www.learntoplaymusic.com

Contact us via email
info@learntoplaymusic.com

Like us on Facebook
www.facebook.com/LearnToPlayMusic

Follow us on Twitter
twitter.com/LTPMusic

View our YouTube Channel
www.youtube.com/learntoplaymusiccom

Published by
KOALA MUSIC PUBLICATIONS™
PROGRESSIVE BEGINNER HARMONICA
ISBN: 978-1-86469-171-9
Order Code: 69171

Acknowledgments
Cover Photograph: Phil Martin
Photographs: Phil Martin

CONTENTS

INTRODUCTION

Progressive Beginner Harmonica assumes you have no prior knowledge of music or playing the Harmonica. It will provide you with an interesting and informative introduction to harmonica playing and teach you many songs and solos in various styles along the way. All the essential sounds and techniques of harmonica playing are presented in the book along with the basics of music as they apply to the harmonica. Each new rhythm, musical concept or technique is introduced with a simple explanation and several musical examples demonstrating each new sound or technique. Topics such as bending notes, train imitation sounds and cross harp Blues playing are discussed in detail. After completing this book you will have a solid understanding of the harmonica and will be ready for further study on specific styles of harmonica playing. The lessons are graded so that your knowledge and technique will develop simultaneously. **All harmonica players should know all of the information contained in this book.**

The best and fastest way to learn is to use this book in conjunction with:

1. Buying sheet music and song books of your favourite recording artists and learning to play their songs.
2. Practicing and playing with other musicians. You will be surprised how good a basic harmonica/guitar or harmonica/piano combination can sound even when playing easy music.
3. Learning by listening to your favourite recordings.

Also in the early stages it is helpful to have the guidance of an experienced teacher. This will also help you keep to a schedule and obtain weekly goals.

USING THE VIDEO AND AUDIO

It's recommended that you use the accompanying video and audio available (see the front of this book for more details). The book explains the techniques to use, while the video and audio lets you see and hear how each example should look and sound when played correctly.

 ◀— This icon with a number indicates that a recorded example is available.

Practice the examples on your own, playing slowly at first. Then try playing with a metronome set to a slow tempo, until you can play the example evenly and without stopping. Gradually increase the tempo as you become more confident and then you can try playing along with the recordings.

SECTION 1
Basic Techniques, Rhythms and Sounds

WHICH HARMONICA TO USE

This book is designed to be used with the **diatonic ten hole harmonica,** which is the most common type of harmonica. It is also the best type for bending notes and several other techniques essential for harmonica playing. There are many different brands of diatonic harmonica available. Some of my personal favorites are the **Hohner marine band** or **special 20** models, and the **Lee Oskar** by **Tombo.** A common variation in types of ten hole harmonica is that the body of the instrument may be made of either wood or plastic. Although some players prefer the wooden body, the plastic version is more practical because it can be washed without any swelling of the body. When the wood swells, the edges of each block can become rough and can cut your mouth. With plastic, this does not happen.The recording which accompanies this book has been recorded with a **C harmonica**. This means that a harmonica with a **C** written on it (as shown below) is tuned to the key of C. The word "key" means the central note to which all others relate. There are twelve different keys used in music and each one begins on a different pitch. To play along with the recording you will need a C harmonica, so make sure your harmonica has a C written somewhere on it.

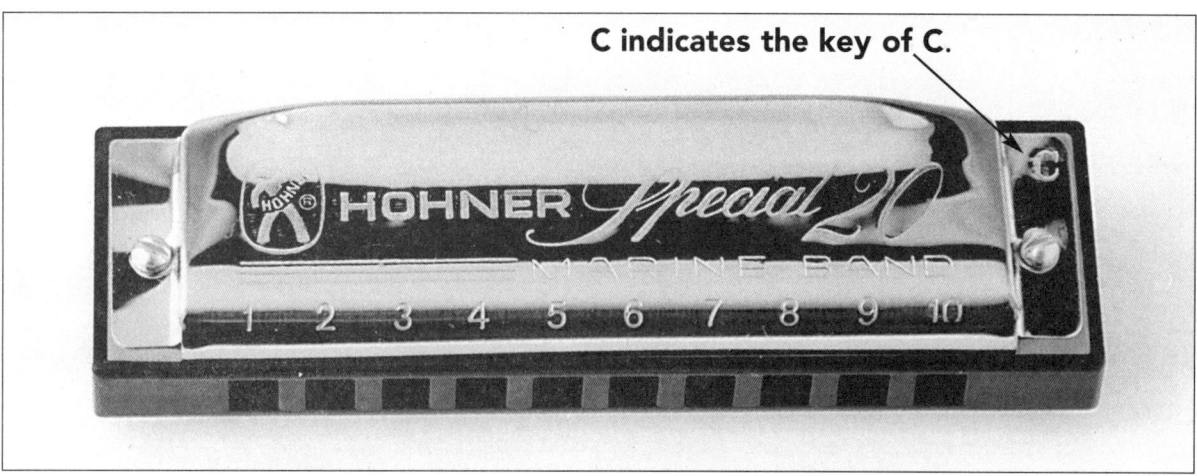

C indicates the key of C.

HOW TO HOLD THE HARMONICA

The best way to hold the harmonica is shown below, using the **left hand**, with the low numbered end of the harmonica held gently between your thumb and forefinger. The numbers on the harmonica should be facing upward. This hand position will prepare you to use the sound effect known as the **hand vibrato** or **wah wah**, which is introduced in lesson 4. It can be used by right or left-handed players alike. Keep the four fingers of the left hand straight, and pressed gently but closely together, with no visible gaps between them.

LESSON ONE

MAKING MUSICAL SOUNDS

The harmonica is capable of producing both **notes and chords**. A **note** is the sound produced by inhaling or exhaling on any one hole of the harmonica. A **chord** is a combination of three or more notes played together. In some situations it is desirable to play **two** notes together. This is called a **double stop**. Each of these possibilities requires a different technique to produce the correct sound. These different methods will be dealt with as the book progresses. The easiest thing to play on the harmonica to begin with is a chord. To locate a particular three hole chord, simply place your mouth at the center note of the chord, allowing your mouth to cover a comfortable amount of the harmonica. For example, to play a chord using the **4**, **5**, and **6** holes, center your mouth on the number **5** hole. The number **4** and **6** holes will automatically be included. If you are unsure what holes you are covering, try placing your tongue in one of the holes, then replace it with your finger and have a look to see which hole it is. After doing this a few times you will soon become familiar with which holes you are sounding.

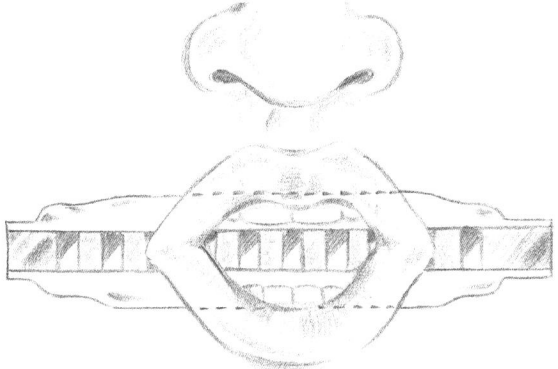

 1.   Low, Middle and High Chords

The first example on the accompanying recording is a demonstration of chords played with exhale and inhale breaths in the low, middle and high sections of the harmonica. To begin the first example, place the harmonica in your mouth centred on hole **2** and exhale. Next, inhale in the same position. After completing the inhaled breath, move further towards the middle of the harmonica and repeat the process, then move to the high end of the harmonica and play again. Don't worry at this stage about exactly what holes you are playing, just get a feeling for where you should move to produce higher or lower sounds. This first example is not notated. Listen to the recording and copy the sounds you hear. As you play, make sure the harmonica points directly into your mouth as shown below rather than being angled. This will allow the air to flow freely through the instrument as you breathe and will produce the clearest sound.

READING THE NOTATION SYSTEM

This book uses a unique harmonica notation system which gives you specific information about which holes to play to get the correct sounds and how long to hold each note for. The system is made up of a combination of numbers corresponding to the holes on the harmonica, and rhythm notation which is closely related to standard musical notation.

The holes on the harmonica are represented by **two types of numbers**.

Outlined numbers indicate notes played with an **inhaled breath**, e.g. 2 indicates the second hole on the harmonica inhaled.

Solid numbers indicate notes played with an **exhaled breath**, e.g. **2** indicates the second hole on the harmonica exhaled.

Chords are indicated by numbers stacked vertically one on top of the other, e.g. 3 2 1 indicates that holes 1, 2 and 3 are played **simultaneously** with an inhale breath.

The length of time a note or chord should sound is indicated by standard musical notes placed under the hole numbers, as shown below.

5 Hole 5 exhaled   6 Hole 6 inhaled

Held for value of **Half note**   Held for value of **Quarter note**

Any **added expression markings** (slides, bends, trills, etc) are placed above the hole numbers in italics, e.g. a bend on hole 4 inhaled would be notated as shown below.

Here is a list of all the expression markings used in the book. Each one of these techniques is introduced individually in the course of the book in the appropriate lesson.

V   Indicates **hand vibrato**

S   Indicates **slide**

B   Indicates **half step bend**

B̄   Indicates **whole step bend**

T   Indicates **trail off**

Tr   Indicates **trill**

W   Indicates **grace note** (mouth wah bend)

BAR LINES

Bar lines are drawn vertically across the notation, which divides the music into sections called **bars** or **measures**. A **double bar line** signifies either the end of the music, or the end of an important section of it.

THE FOUR FOUR TIME SIGNATURE

 These two numbers are called the **four four time signature.** They are placed at the beginning of standard music notation. The ⁴⁄₄ time signature tells you there are four beats in each bar. There are **four** quarter notes in one bar of music in ⁴⁄₄ time.

THE QUARTER NOTE

 This music note is called a **quarter note**. It lasts for **one** beat. There are four quarter notes in one bar of ⁴⁄₄ time.

Count 1

 2. Quarter Notes, The Repeat Sign

This example contains chords played in quarter notes exhaling and inhaling on holes 1, 2 and 3. As you play the example, all of your air should be directed through your mouth and harmonica, with none escaping through your nose, or around the corners of your mouth. Tap your foot and count mentally as you play to help make sure that all the notes are of equal length. The two dots just before the double bar at the end of this example are called a repeat sign and indicate that the example is to be played again from the beginning.

Repeat Sign

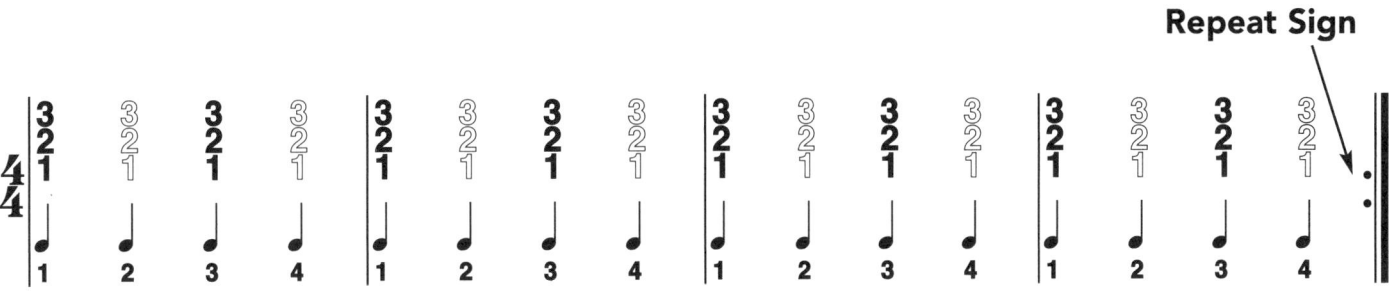

THE WHOLE NOTE

o

Count: **1** 2 3 4

This is a **whole note**. It lasts for **four** beats.
There is **one** whole note in one bar of 4/4 time.
The whole note is the longest note commonly used in music.

 ## 3. Whole Notes

Once again, count mentally and tap your foot as you play to help you keep time.

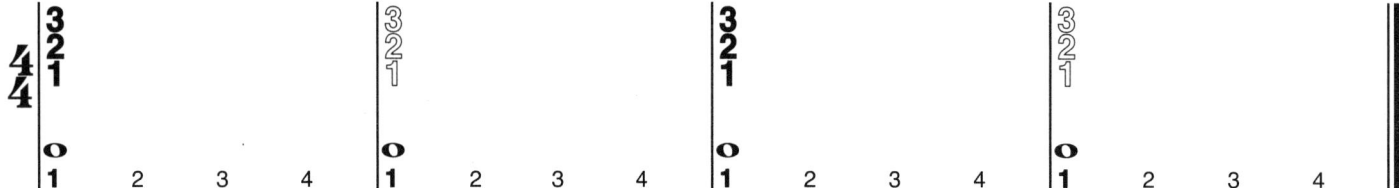

THE HALF NOTE

This music note is called a **half note**. It has a value of **two** beats.
There are **two** half notes in one bar of 4/4 time.

Count **1** 2

 ## 4. Half Notes

CONSECUTIVE BREATHS

Many times in harmonica playing you will find situations where you play chords or notes which require the use of consecutive inhale or exhale breaths. Because we naturally breathe in, out and in again, this can be difficult at first. In the following example, chords are played in quarter, half and whole notes with consecutive exhale breaths and consecutive inhale breaths.

 5.

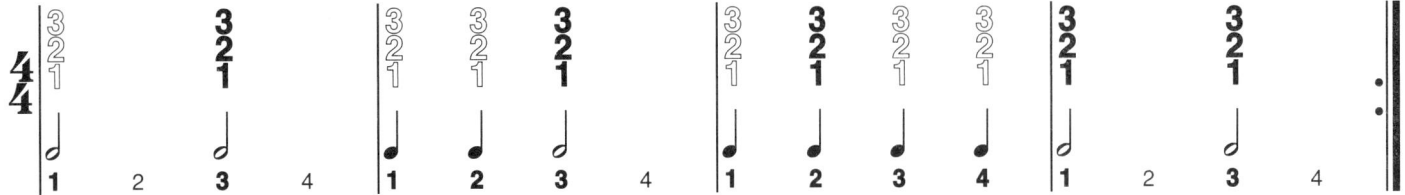

 6.

This example contains a combination of consecutive and alternate **exhale** and **inhale** breaths. Take it slowly at first if necessary.

LESSON TWO

RESTS

Rests are used to indicate silence in music. There are different rests for different lengths of silence just as notes indicate different lengths of sound. The symbols below are very similar. The difference is that the **half rest** sits **on top of the line**, while the **whole rest** hangs **below the line**. The **half rest** indicates **two beats of silence**. The **whole rest** indicates **four beats or a whole bar of silence**. Small counting numbers are placed under rests.

Half Rest	**Whole Rest**
Count 1 2	Count 1 2 3 4

 ## 7. Whole and Half Rests

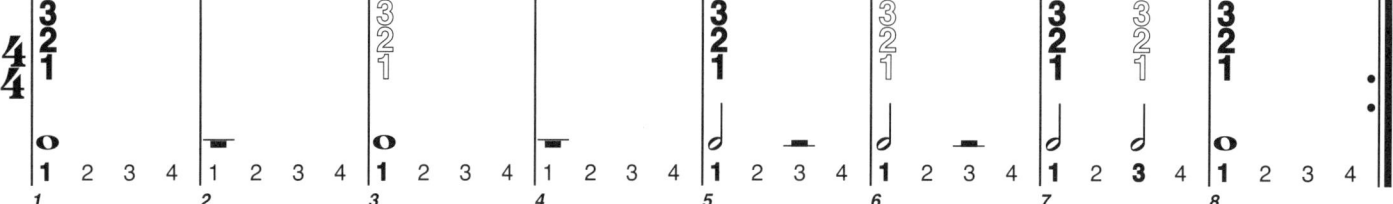

MOVING BETWEEN POSITIONS

So far, everything you have played has been on the lowest three holes of the harmonica. The following example moves between this position and a position one hole further up where your mouth is covering holes **2**, **3** and **4**. Another important thing to notice here is that rests give you a natural place to take a breath if you need it. Try to get into the habit of breathing where rests occur, rather than in between written notes.

 ## 8.

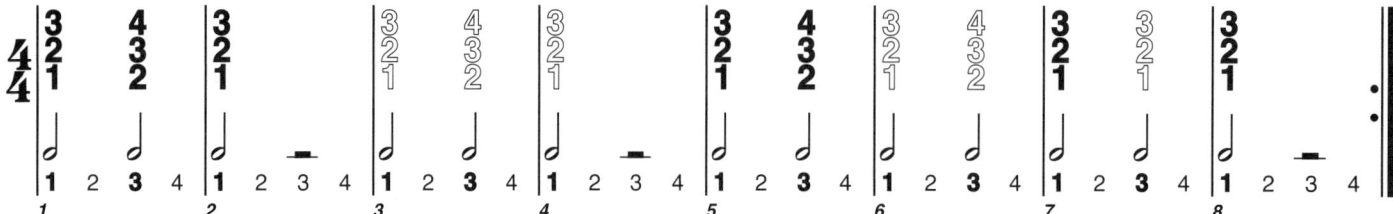

PLAYING SONGS

Here is the first part of the popular children's song **Three Blind Mice**. Playing this song requires several changes of mouth position. Once again, take it slowly at first and breathe where rests occur.

 **9. Three Blind Mice**

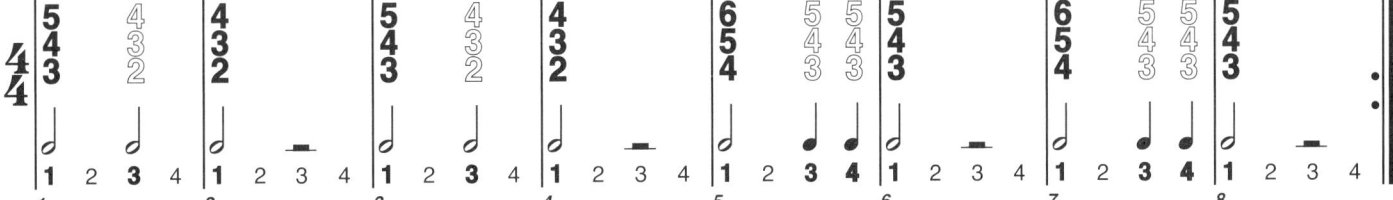

THE QUARTER REST

 This symbol is a **quarter rest.** It indicates **one beat of silence**. Do not play any note. Remember that small counting numbers are placed under rests.

Count   1

The following song makes use of the quarter rest. Once again the rest provides an opportunity to breath without disrupting the flow of the music. Because the quarter rest lasts for only one beat, you will need to be quicker with your breath to make sure you play the next note or chord in time.

Be sure to count and tap your foot as you play. This will help you keep time regardless of whether notes or rests occur in the notation.

 10. Merrily We Roll Along

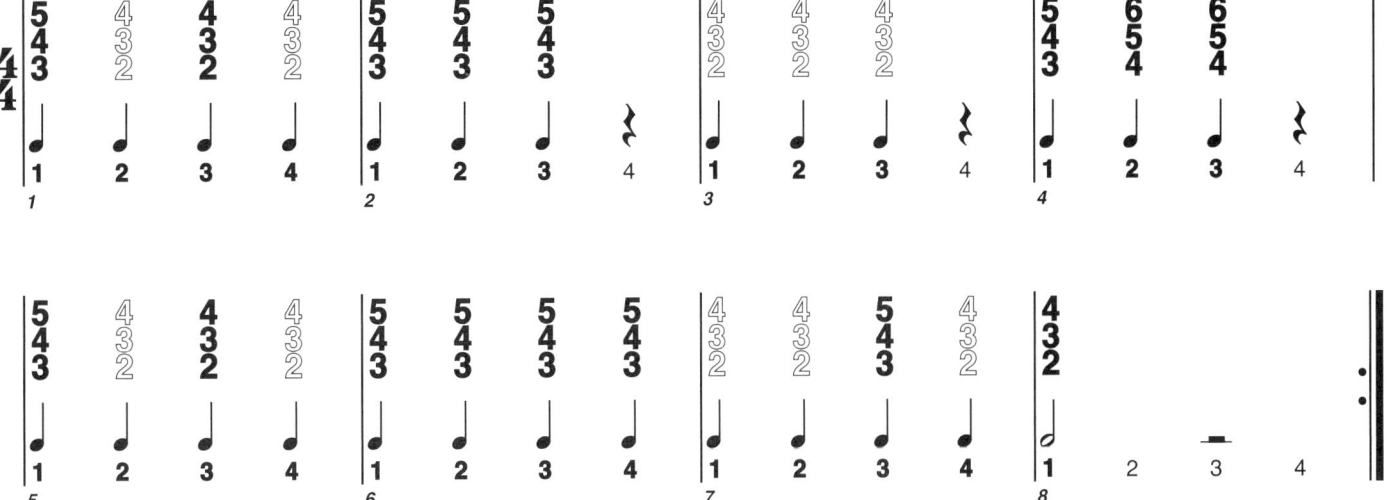

LESSON THREE

PLAYING SINGLE NOTES

Playing single notes is often difficult at first. Most people will still have a second note sounding the first time they attempt single notes. In time the muscles around your lips will develop and single notes will be easy to play, but don't be surprised if you have trouble at first. To play a single note, tighten the muscles that circle your mouth to form a round hole as pictured below. The mouth position used is similar to that used for whistling. Although some tension is required to produce single notes, your eventual goal should be to have all muscles as relaxed as possible, using only the minimum pressure necessary.

The easiest hole to begin playing single notes on is number **1** at the low end of the harmonica. This is because you only have to block the unwanted extra notes on one side of the hole.

 11.

This example demonstrates the difference between single notes on hole **1** and chords.

 **12.**

Here, only single notes are used. These are the notes produced by exhaling and inhaling on hole **1**. The names of these notes are C and D. Since there are no rests in this example, the best place to take a breath is at the end of each whole note. This is common when playing melodies.

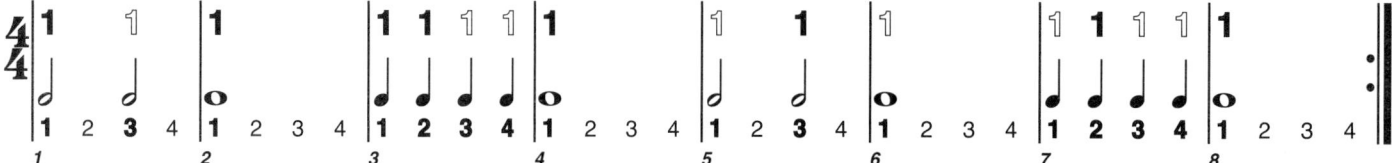

 **13.**

Once you are confident with the previous example, try this one which moves between holes **4** and **3**. Because these notes have other notes either side of them this may be more difficult, so be patient and keep practicing and you will soon have it under control.

 14. Three Blind Mice - Version 2

Here is the first part of **Three Blind Mice** played in single notes. Don't worry if you are finding it difficult to produce single notes clearly without extra notes sounding at this stage. This is very common. It takes time for your lips and facial muscles to develop, so practice often but for short periods. Soon you will have single notes well under control and you will be able to play many melodies.

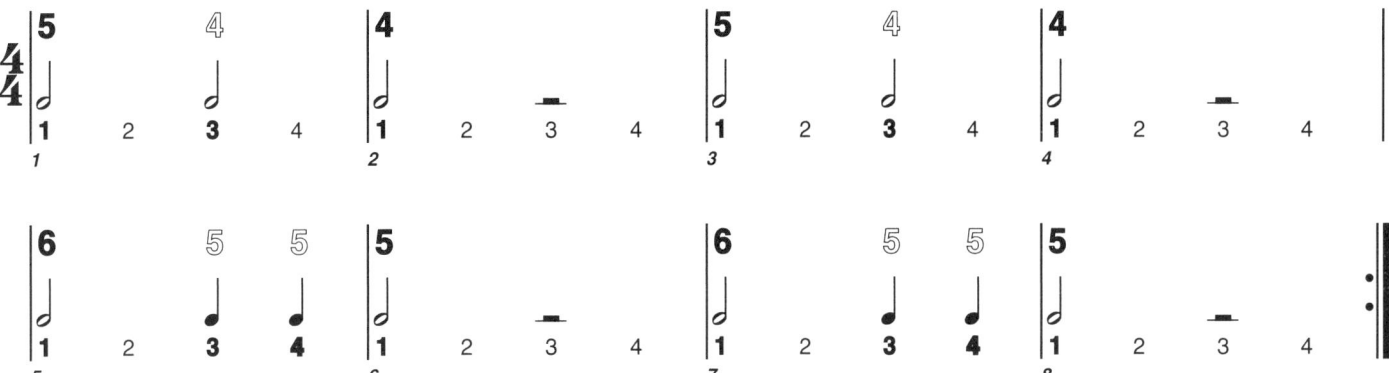

 15. Ode to Joy

This popular melody is the main theme to Beethoven's ninth Symphony.

THE THREE FOUR TIME SIGNATURE

This time signature is called the **three four** time signature. It tells you there are **three** beats in each bar. Three four time is also known as waltz time. There are **three** quarter notes in one bar of ¾ time.

THE DOTTED HALF NOTE

Count 1 2 3

A **dot** written after a note extends its value by **half**.
A dot after a half note means that you hold it for **three** beats.
One dotted half note makes one bar of music in ¾ time.

The following song **Beautiful Brown Eyes** is a typical example of the way dotted half notes are used in ¾ time. As there are no rests in the first three lines of this example, you could breathe at the end of any of the dotted half notes if you need to. Listen as you play each song and try to find the most natural sounding places to breathe. The final bar of this song contains a whole rest. In ¾ time, a whole rest indicates a whole bar rest.

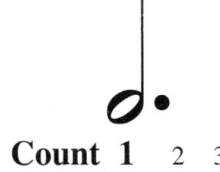

16. Beautiful Brown Eyes

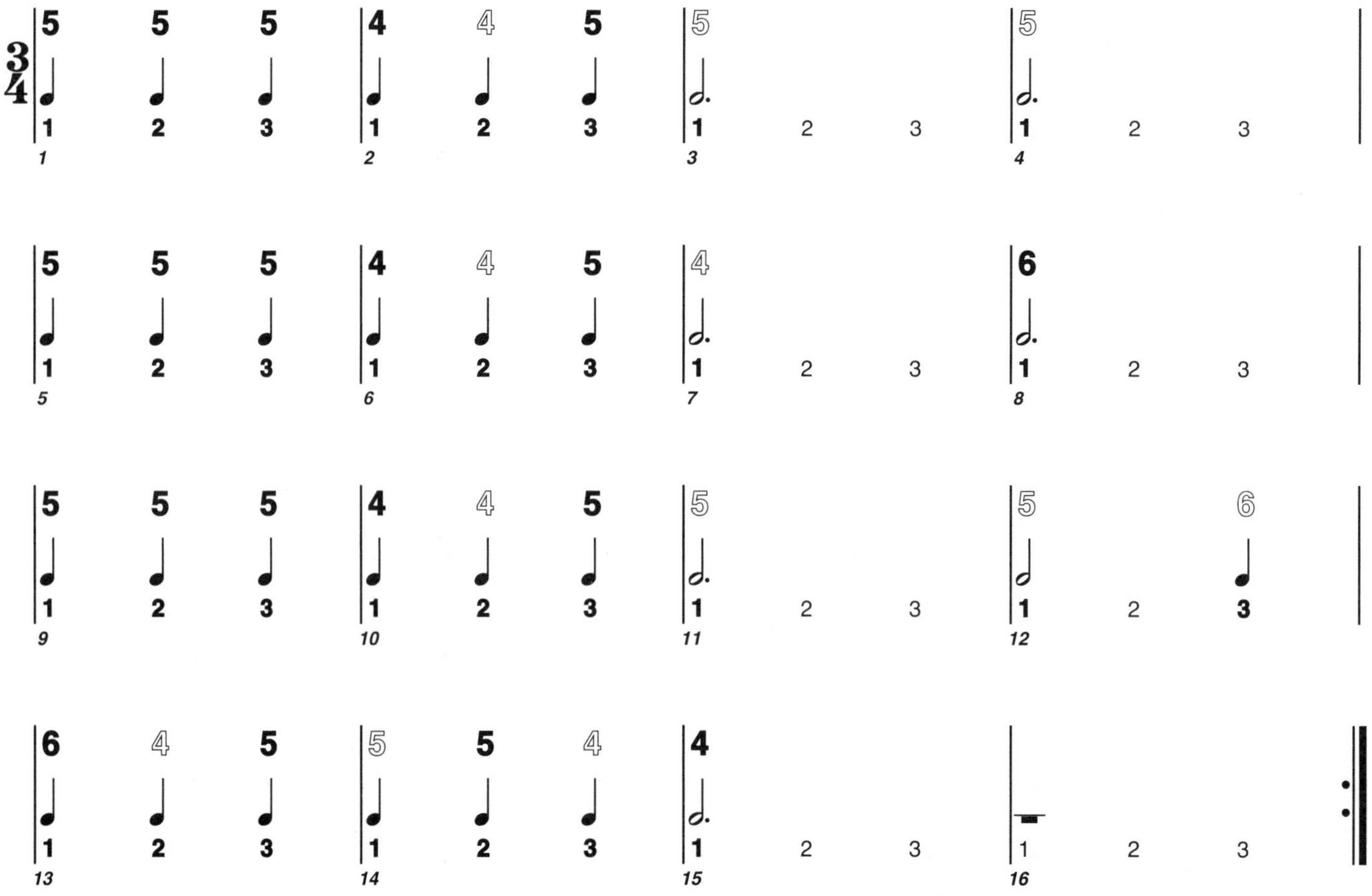

 ## 17. Minor Mood

Here is another song in ¾ time. This one has a sad kind of tonality known as a **minor key**. This term will be dealt with in lesson 12. Don't be too concerned with the terminology for now, just be aware that each different kind of sound has a name in music. If you are curious, ask a musical friend or music teacher about each of the terms you encounter here.

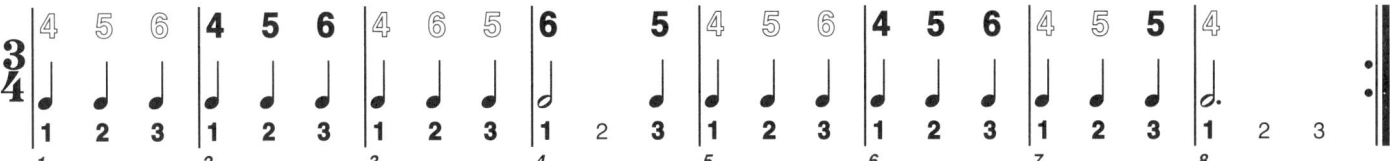

THE LEAD-IN

Sometimes a song does not begin on the first beat of a bar. Any notes which come before the first full bar are called **lead-in notes** (or pick-up notes). When lead-in notes are used, the last bar is also incomplete. The notes in the lead-in and the notes in the last bar add up to one full bar. The following song is an early Jazz standard made popular by brass bands in New Orleans. It contains **three lead-in notes**. On the recording there are **five** drumbeats to introduce this song.

 ## 18. When the Saints go Marchin' in

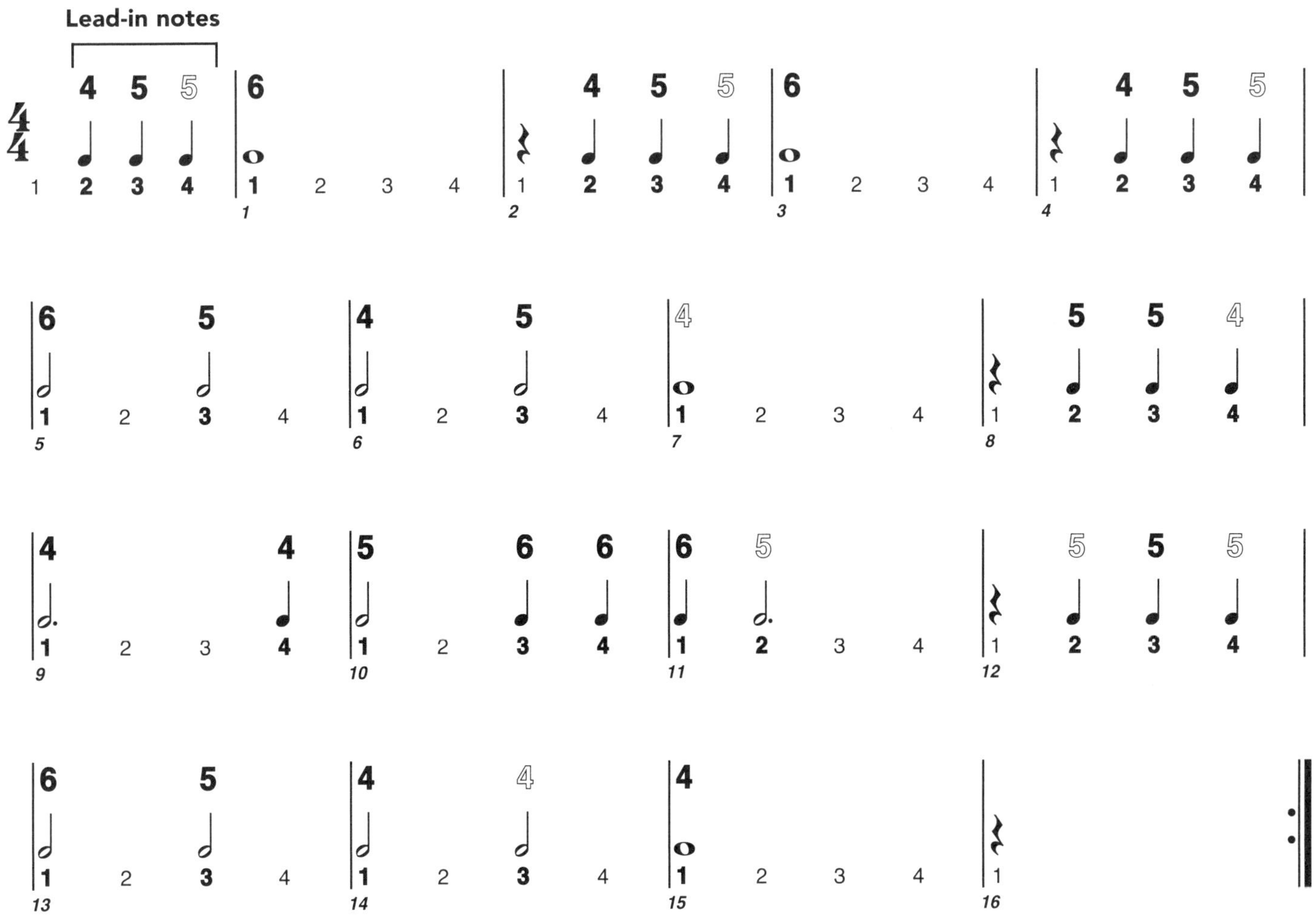

LESSON FOUR

HAND VIBRATO

Hand vibrato or "wah wah" is an effect which is used to add expression to harmonica playing. If you have ever seen a good harmonica player, it is likely that you have seen them using this technique. To somebody watching, it looks like the player is waving or fluttering one hand back and forth while holding the harmonica with the other. The hand vibrato alters the flow of air through the harmonica, thus altering the sound. When playing the hand vibrato, the right hand is moving between two basic positions. The first is formed by cupping the right hand around the left in its normal holding position, as shown in the diagram below. The heels of both hands should be touching and the right hand fingers should curl up along the left hand little finger and around and upwards past the end of the left hand little finger and ring finger. This position results in the air being closed off by the two hands.

To complete the movement for the hand vibrato, the right wrist is swivelled slightly around to the right. This results in the "cup" being opened up and allowing air through. The wrist can then be swivelled back to the left to close the cup again. It is this movement back and forth that causes the vibrato or wah wah effect to sound. The hand vibrato is indicated in the notation by a **V** above the note or chord to which it applies. Experiment with slow, medium and fast vibrato. There is no right or wrong speed for this technique, as different approaches will sound best in different musical situations. Listen to example 19 to hear a demonstration of hand vibrato.

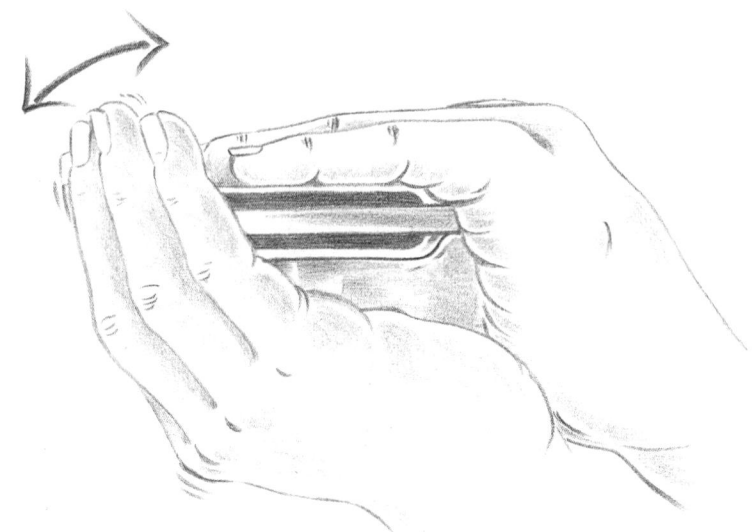

19. Hand Vibrato

This example uses the hand vibrato on both notes and chords. Listen to the recording to hear the difference between notes played without vibrato and notes played with vibrato.

 ## 20. Banks of the Ohio

The most common place the hand vibrato is used is on sustained notes such as whole notes, as demonstrated in this example. Try using the hand vibrato on other tunes you have learnt.

THE TRAIN WHISTLE

A common sound effect which makes use of the wah wah sound is the **train whistle**. As you play the following example, actually mouth the words **wah wah** at the same time as you use the hand wah wah technique. This will also prepare you for other harmonica techniques introduced later in the book.

 **21.**

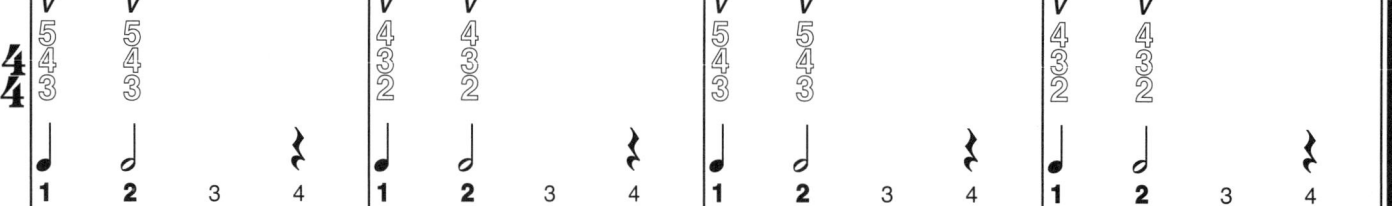

THE TIE

The following example demonstrates the use of **ties**. A **tie** is a curved line which connects two different notes of the same pitch. The tie tells you to play the **first** note only, and to hold it for the length of both notes. A tie may occur either **across a bar line**, or **within one bar**. The use of ties is the only way of indicating that a note or chord is to be held across a bar line. Don't forget to count as you play so you know how long you have held each note for.

 22.

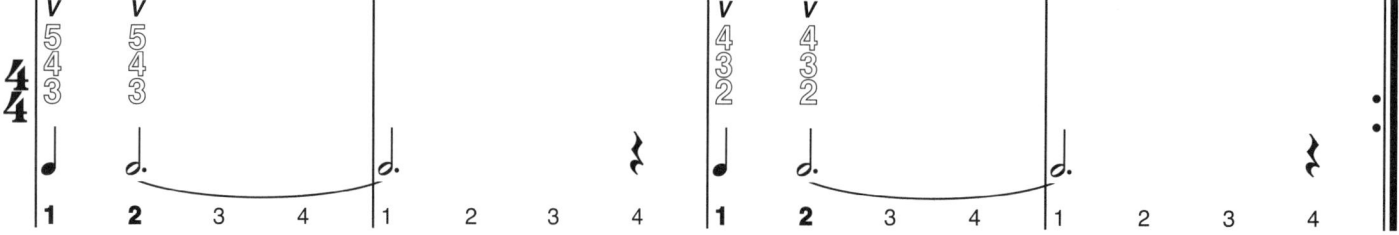

 23.

This example combines the train whistle with a simple train rhythm. The harmonica is a great instrument for imitating the sounds of the steam train. There is a whole tradition of this style of playing and if you can do it, you will be sure to have everybody's feet moving!

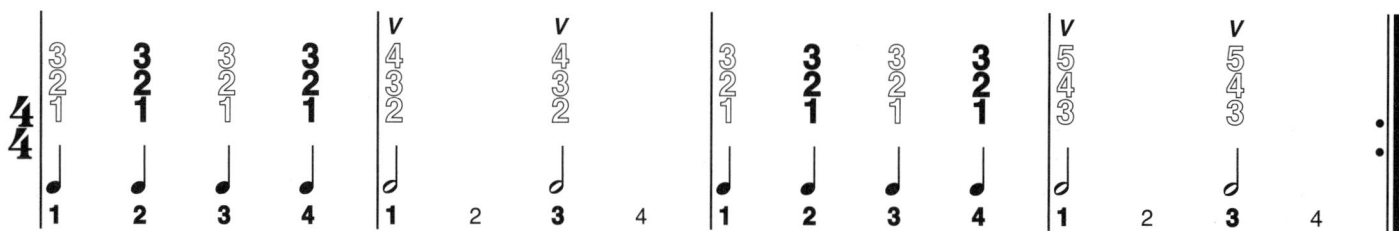

COMBINING CHORDS AND SINGLE NOTES

The next step in developing the train rhythm is to combine chords and single notes, specifically the hole 1 **inhale** note. There are also many other musical situations where you will need to alternate between chords and single notes, so take your time and learn this example carefully.

 24.

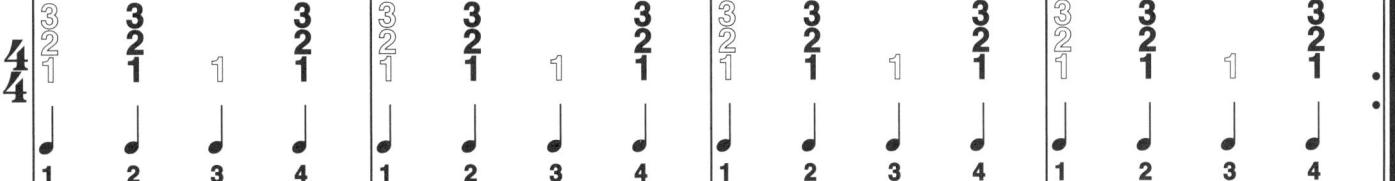

 25. I Hear the Train a Comin'

Now try this solo which makes use of all the train sounds you have learnt. Take it slowly at first and then build up speed as you become more confident.

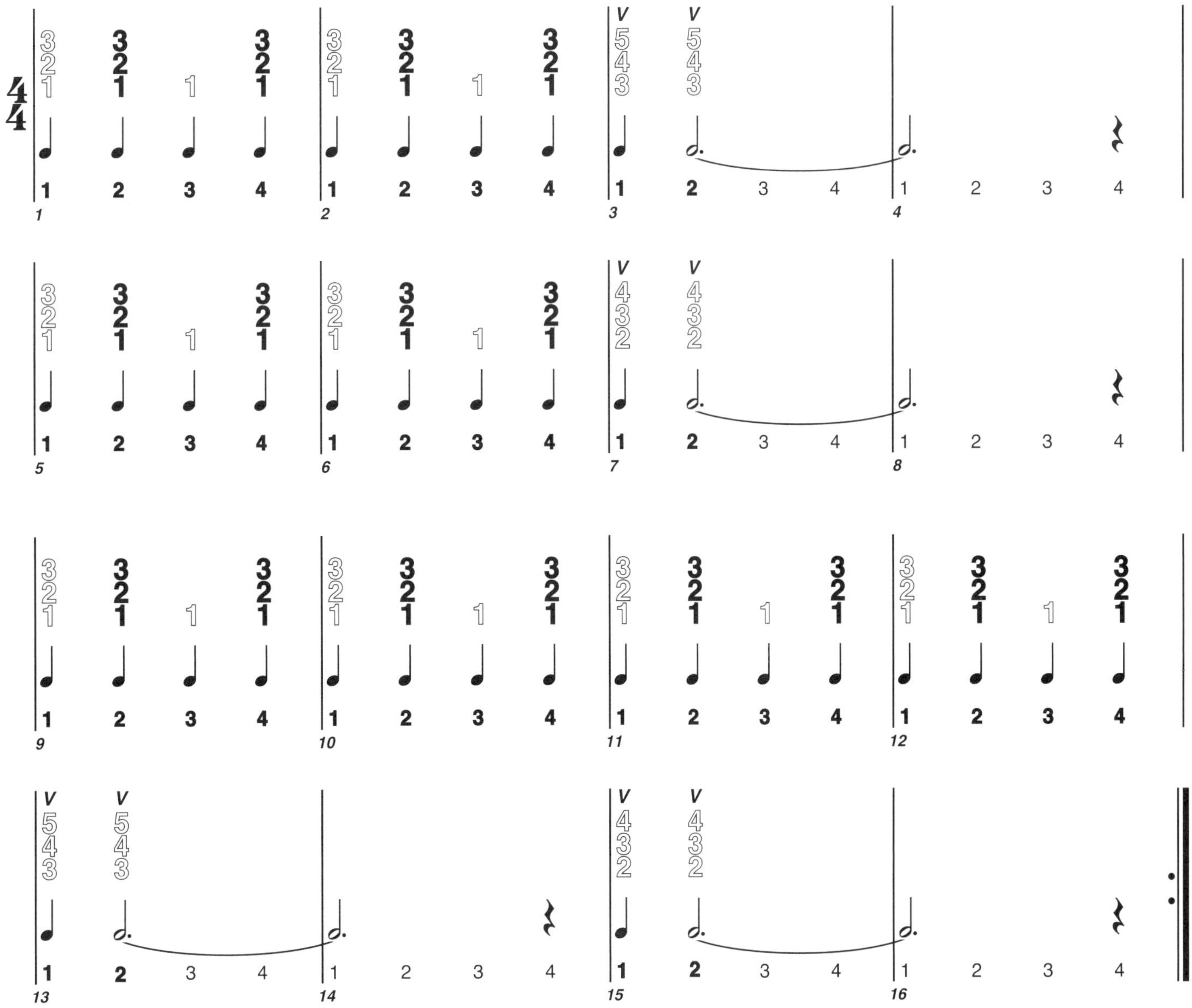

TONGUING

Everything you have played up to this point has been done by simply inhaling or exhaling through the harmonica. However, there are several other techniques used to produce notes on the harmonica. The most important of these is tonguing. This means articulating the sound of each note with the tongue by saying **ta** as you play. Listen to the following example on the recording to hear the difference between notes and chords played without the tongue and then with the tongue.

26.

27.

Here is a single note exercise to help you become more confident with the tonguing technique. Remember to say **ta ta ta ta** to get the correct sound when tonguing.

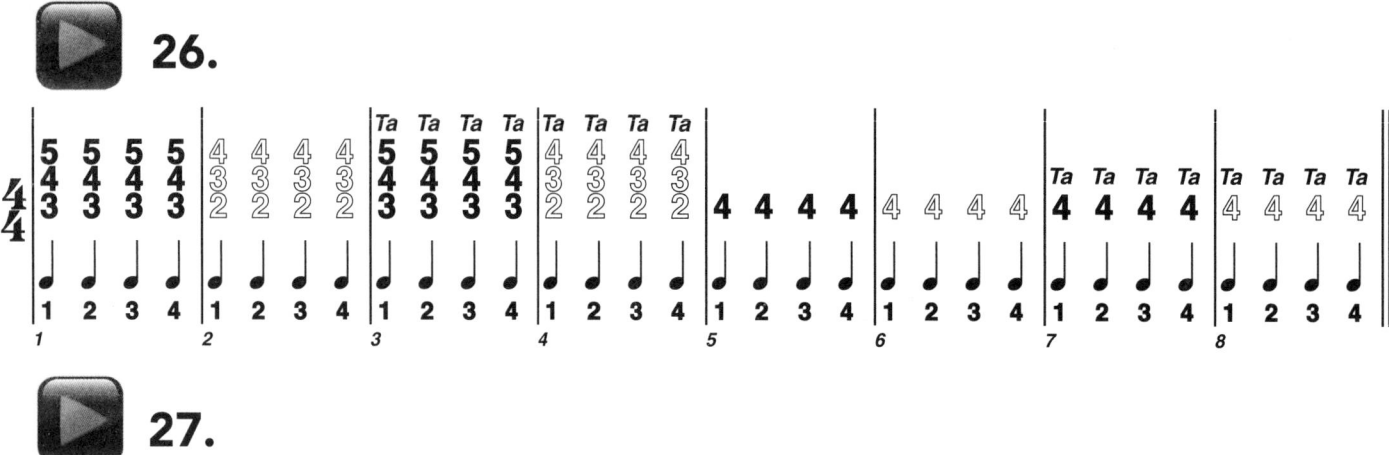

SECTION 2
More Complex Rhythms, Scales, Blues Playing

LESSON FIVE

THE EIGHTH NOTE

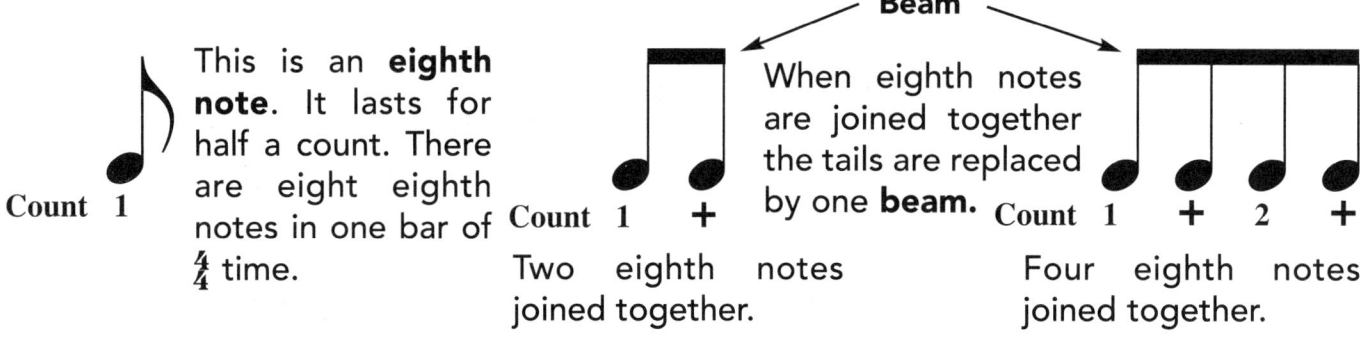

Count 1 — This is an **eighth note**. It lasts for half a count. There are eight eighth notes in one bar of 4/4 time.

Count 1 + — Two eighth notes joined together.

Beam — When eighth notes are joined together the tails are replaced by one **beam**.

Count 1 + 2 + — Four eighth notes joined together.

 ## 28. How to Count Eighth Notes

 ## 29. Lavender's Blue

Eighth notes occur in 3/4 time as well as 4/4 time. Remember to count mentally and tap your foot as you play. Take this one slowly at first.

STACCATO

A dot placed above or below a note tells you to play the note **staccato.** Staccato means to play a note short and separate from other notes. There are two ways to play a note staccato. If you are tonguing the note, make a "**dot**" sound with your tongue. If you are not tonguing the note, make a "**huck**" sound with the back of your tongue. Both these methods cut off the flow of air, thus stopping the note short.

 30.

 31. Shortnin' Bread

This popular children's song demonstrates the way staccato notes may be used in a melody.

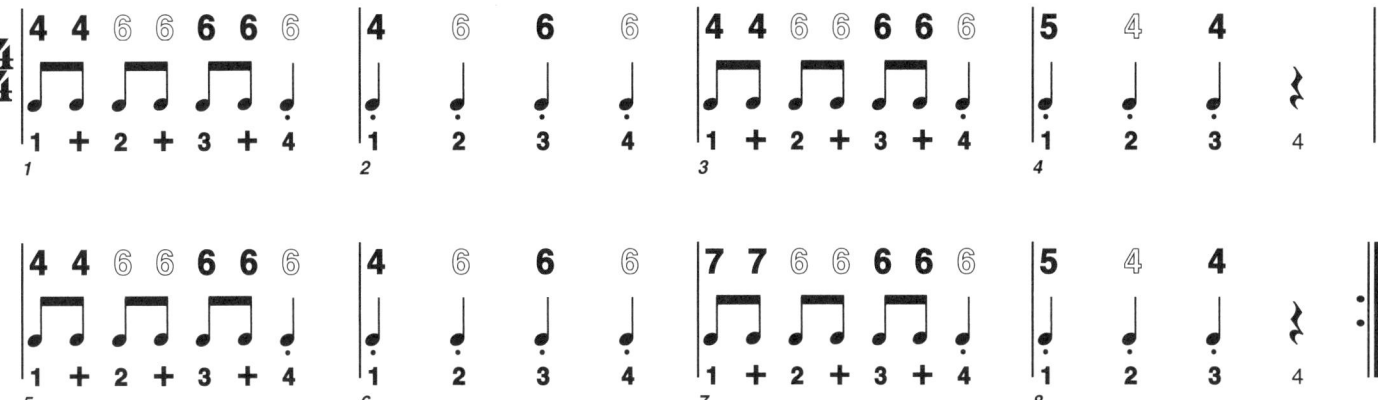

DOUBLE TONGUING

Another useful technique for articulating notes is called double tonguing. This technique is used by many wind instrument players and is just as valuable on the harmonica as it is on the trumpet or saxophone, **especially when playing train rhythms**. Double tonguing means playing each group of two notes with a "**ta ka**" sound. The first note is articulated with the front of the tongue (**ta**) and the second note is articulated with the back of the tongue. Try saying **taka taka taka taka** several times before playing the following example.

 32.

 **33.**

Here is a variation containing ties which is also useful for playing train rhythms. Take it slowly at first.

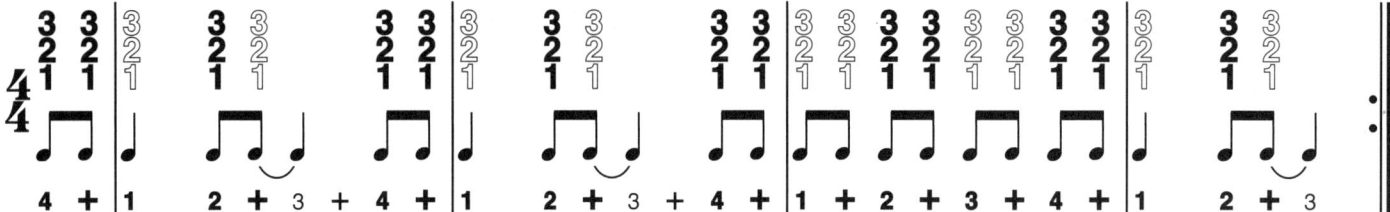

 **34. Freight Train Stomp**

Here is another train solo complete with whistles, making use of the techniques you have just learnt.

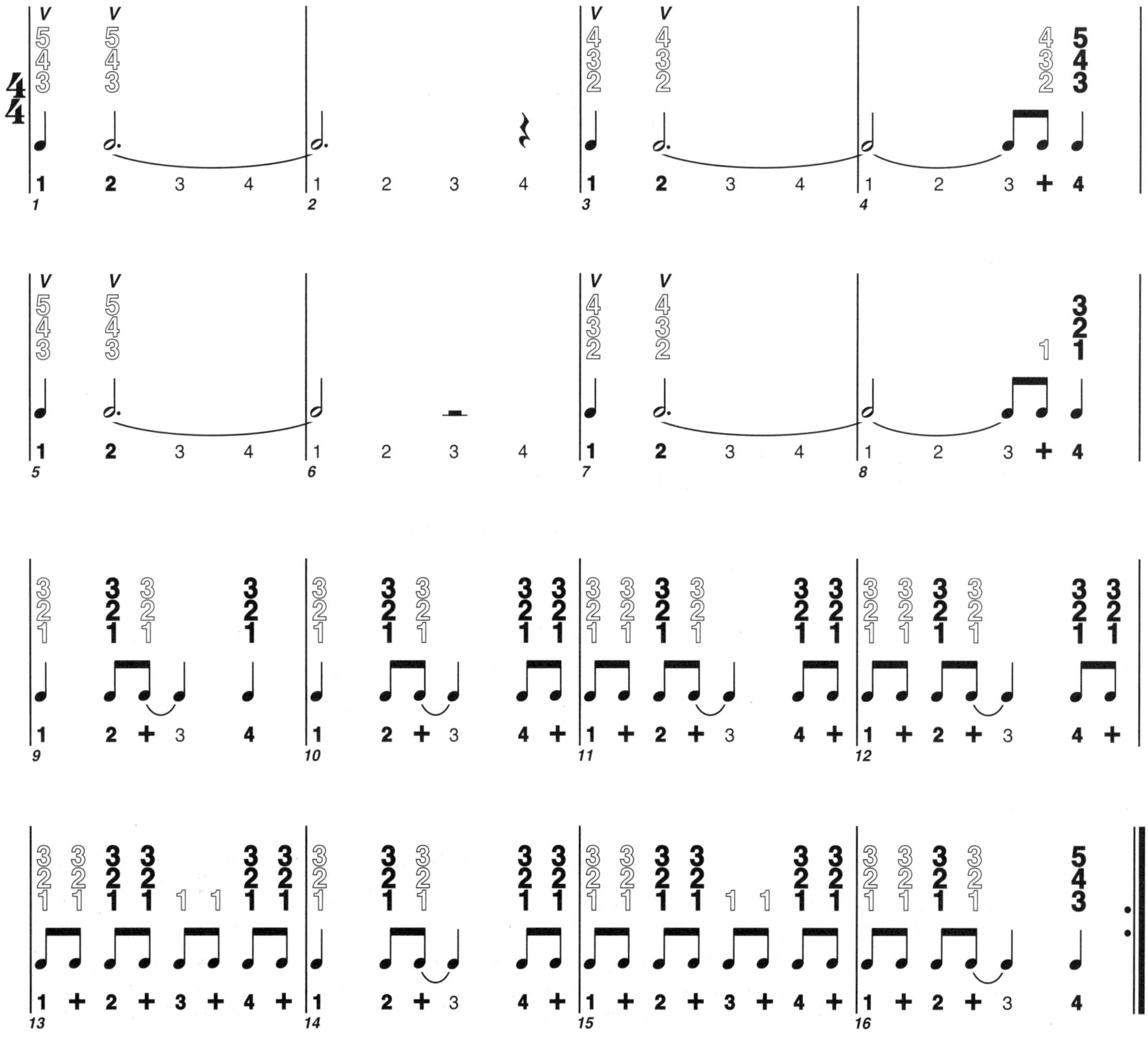

LESSON SIX

12 BAR BLUES

12 Bar Blues is a pattern of chords which repeats every 12 bars. There are hundreds of well known songs based on this chord progression, i.e., they contain basically the same chords in the same order. 12 bar Blues is one of the most common progressions in Blues, Jazz and Rock. Every harmonica player will be regularly asked to play a 12 bar Blues. In fact it is very likely to be the first kind of song used at any jam session. The following example demonstrates a common 12 bar Blues riff played on the harmonica. A **riff** is a pattern of notes which repeats and may be altered slightly to fit the chords.

 35. 12 Bar Blues

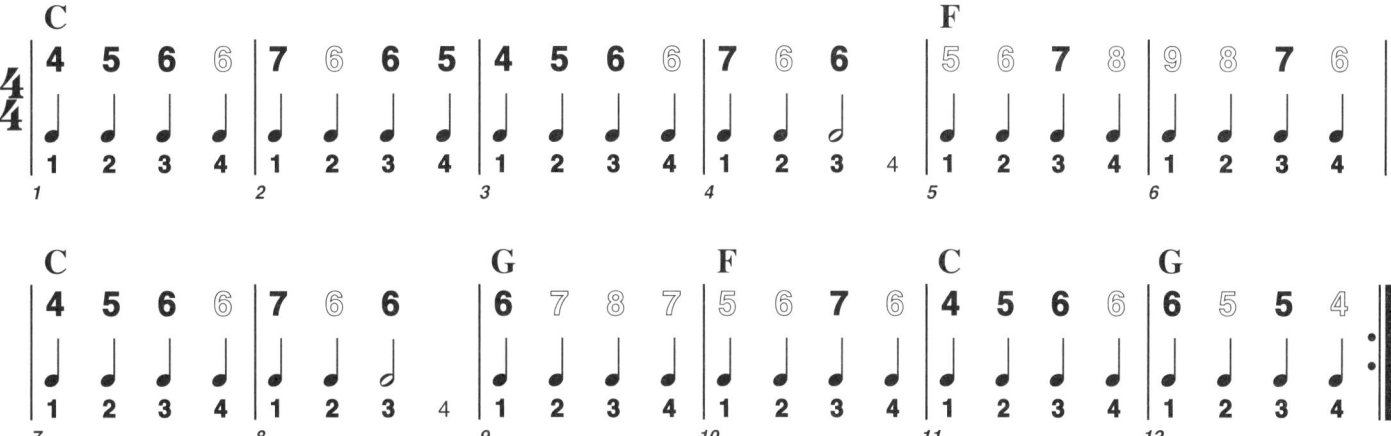

One of the classic sounds in Blues music is the combination of harmonica and guitar. When you play any riff or melody on a 12 bar Blues progression, your notes are fitting in with a specific set of chords which can be played by a guitar (or keyboard). The chords most commonly played by the guitar are built on the first, fourth and fifth notes of the key you are playing in. These chords are often described by the use of roman numerals. If you are playing in the key of C, these chords will be C (Ī), F (ĪV̄) and G (V̄). A detailed explanation of notes and chords as scale degrees is given in lessons 11 and 12. The easiest way to start recognising the relationship between notes and chords is to remember that each time you begin playing a riff on a C note (hole **1**, **4** or **7** exhale), the guitar will most likely be playing a **C chord**, which is simply the C note with two additional notes on top of it. When the note and chord are played together, a harmonious sound is produced. In the following examples, chord symbols for the chords C, F and G are written above the notation to show which chords a guitar would play to accompany the harmonica. The basic pattern of the 12 bar Blues is shown below.

Ī	Ī	Ī	Ī
ĪV̄	ĪV̄	Ī	Ī
V̄	ĪV̄	Ī	V̄

 **36.**

Here is a variation on the previous 12 bar Blues riff, this time using eighth notes. Since there are no long notes in this example, you will need to take a quick breath at the end of every second bar.

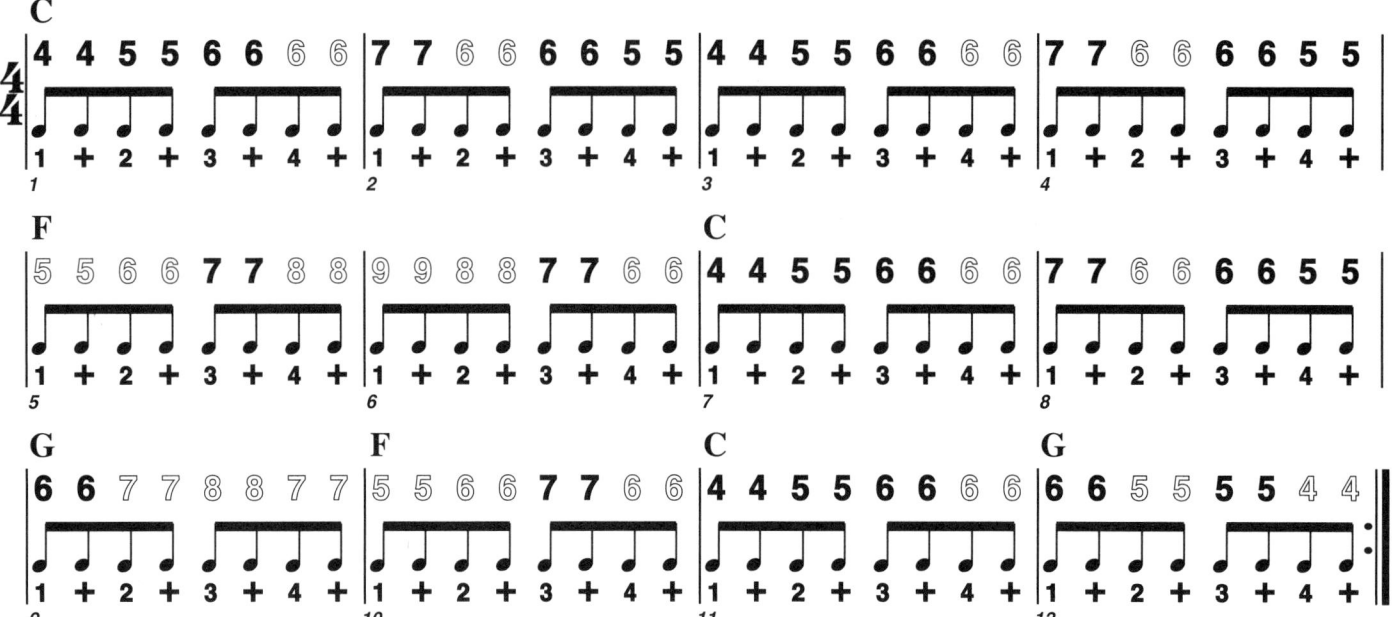

THE EIGHTH REST

 This is an **eighth rest**.
It indicates **half a beat of silence**.

 37.

All the chords in this example are played on the **and** (**+**) part of the count.

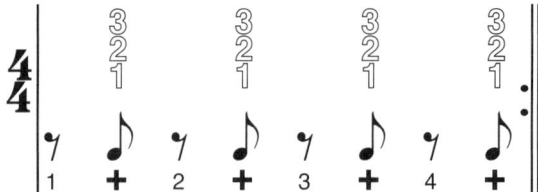

 **38.**

This 12 bar Blues makes use of both quarter and eighth rests. The only notes in this example are **C**, **F** and **G**, which are the notes on which the chords for a 12 bar Blues in the key of C are built.

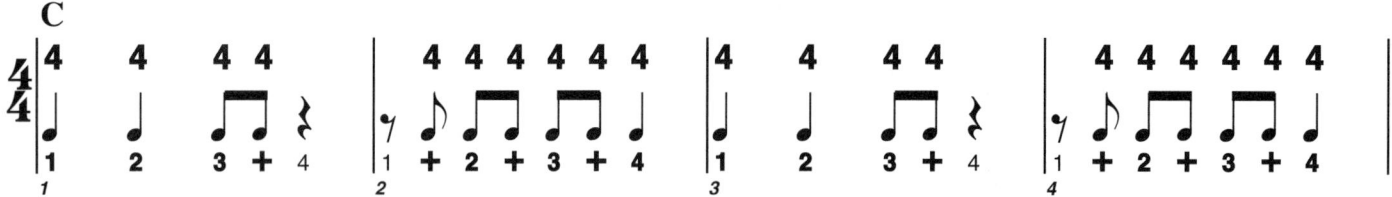

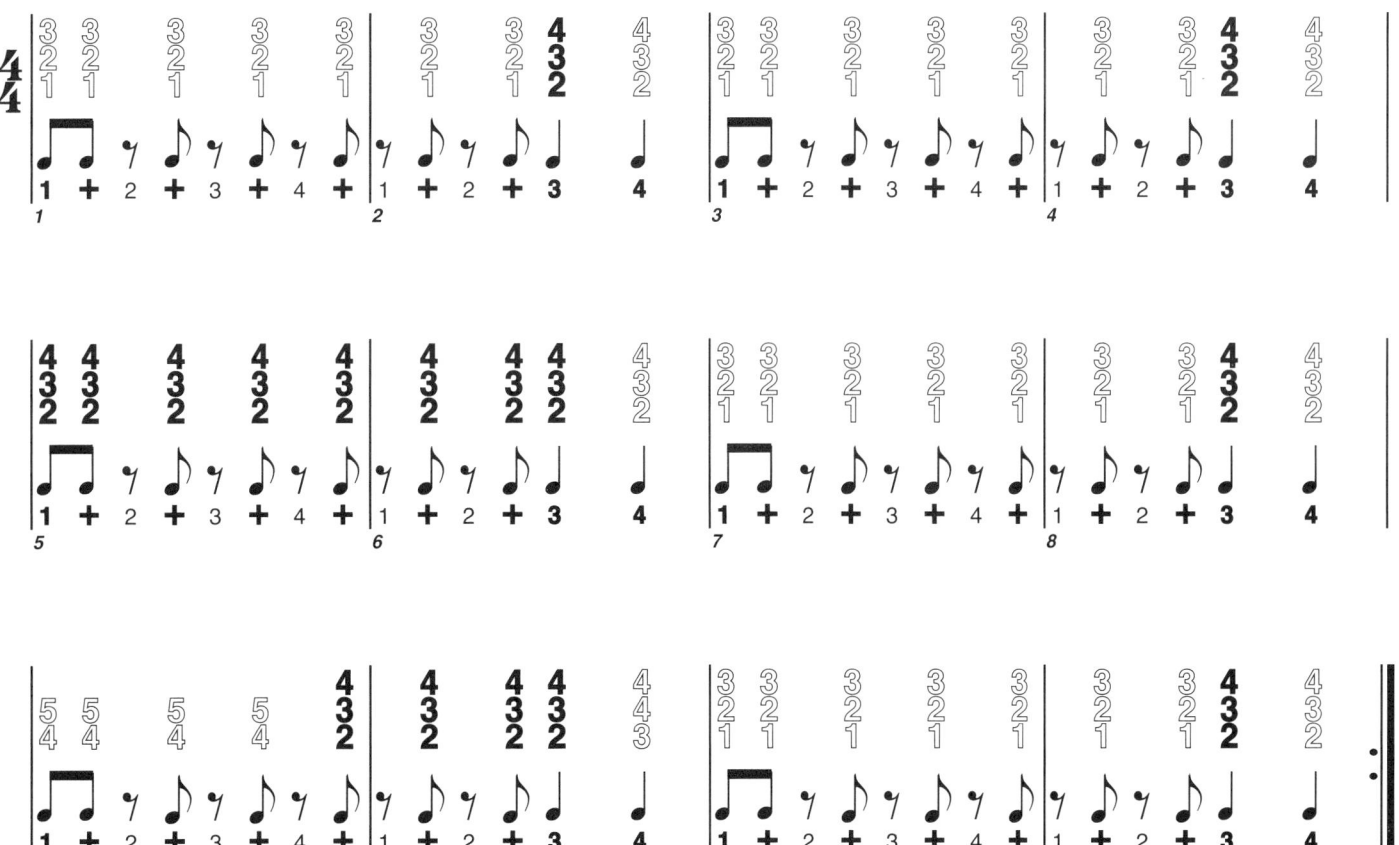

39.

Here is another 12 bar Blues using eighth rests. This one is a rhythm part which works well with a guitar or a whole band.

CROSS HARP PLAYING

On any harmonica, it is possible to play in more than one key even though there is a specific key written on the harmonica. This is because there are a variety of different sounds used in music and the "major scale" (see lesson 7 on the following page) is only one of these sounds. The most common way of playing in another key is to use what is called **second position** or **cross harp**. This method is essential for Blues playing and is also used for other styles such as Country and Rock. When you play cross harp on the C harmonica, C is no longer the key note. The note G now becomes the key note. The note G can be found at holes 2, **3**, **6** and **9** (see lesson 11 for detailed description). This method of playing can take some time to get used to, but is essential if you wish to pursue techniques such as note bending. The train imitation sounds you have already played have been cross harp in the key of G, so you're halfway there already! If you are playing a 12 bar Blues in the key of G, the guitar would be playing the chords G (Ī), C (ĪV) and D (V̄). On page 60 there is a chart showing which key harmonica to choose for cross harp playing with every key used in music. The following 12 bar Blues in the key of G uses the cross harp position to play a riff based around the notes G, C and D which are the **root** (foundation) notes of the chords played by the guitar to accompany the harmonica.

 40. 12 Bar Blues in the Key of G

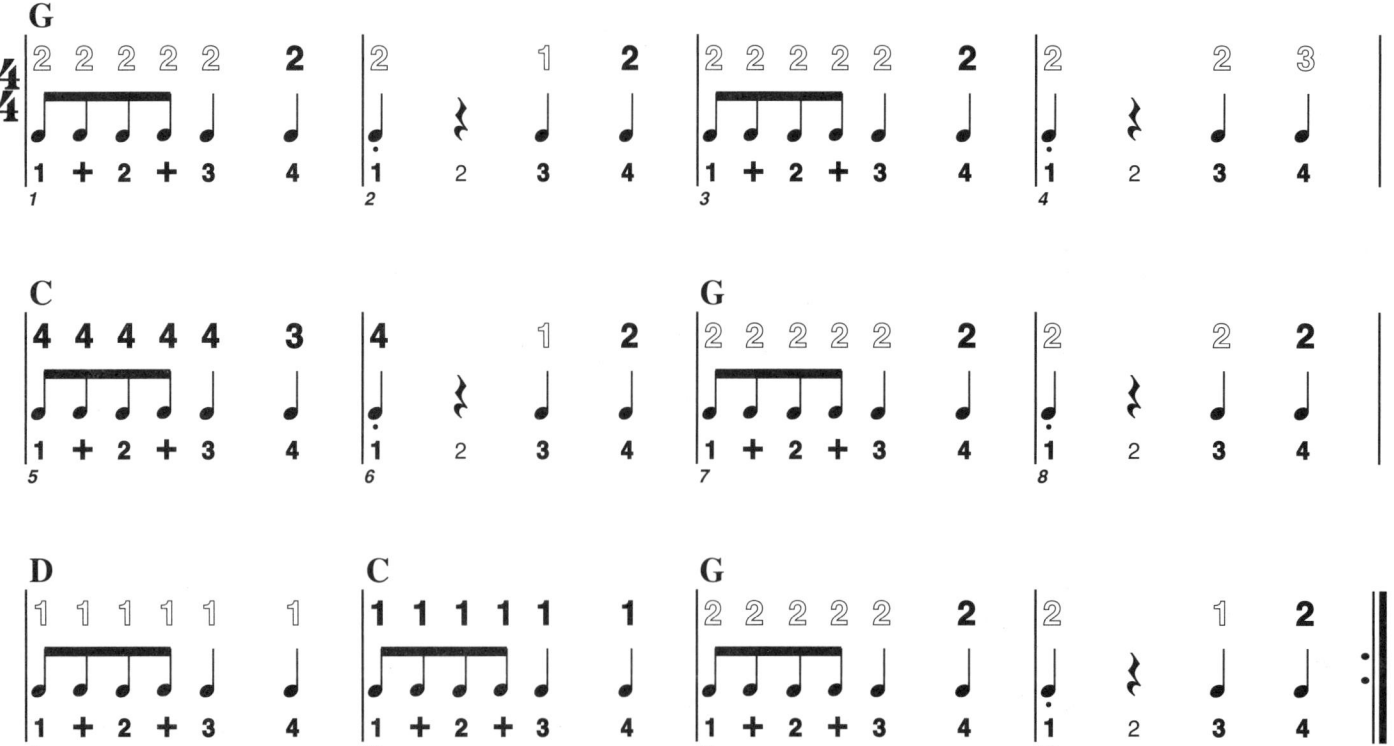

LESSON SEVEN

THE C MAJOR SCALE

The **Major Scale** is a series of eight notes in alphabetical order that has the familiar sound:

DO   RE   MI   FA   SO   LA   TI   DO

The notes of the major scale are easy to find on the harmonica. You have already played many tunes derived from the C major scale. The following example demonstrates the sound of the C major both ascending and descending. It is worth memorising the pattern of holes used to produce the major scale. This helps to identify how to play sounds by ear, which is an important part of harmonica playing. The scale starts on hole **4** and continues up to **7**. It mostly consists of an exhale breath followed by an inhale breath, except for the notes La (6) and Ti (7) which are both inhale breaths. When you reach the higher Do (**7**) you have played **one octave** of the major scale. An octave is the range of 8 notes of the major scale. The lower and higher Do are said to be one octave apart.

 41. C Major Scale

The C major scale consists of the following notes.

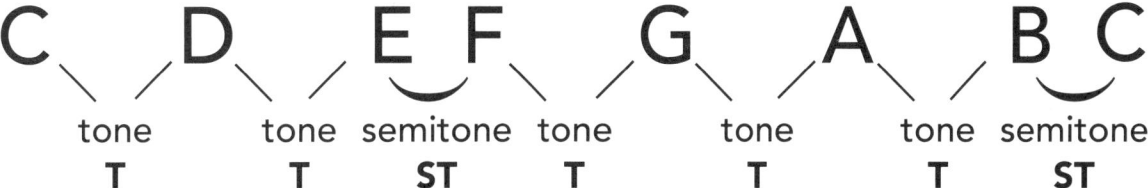

The distances between the notes are measured in tones (or whole steps) and semitones (or half steps). These are the basic building blocks for scales in all keys. As the terms would suggest, a tone or whole step is made up of two semitones or half steps. An understanding of whole and half steps becomes more important when it comes to note bending (discussed in lesson 9) as these are the two possible distances notes are usually bent on the harmonica.

 42.

Here is an exercise to help you become more familiar with the C major scale. It consists mostly of groups of two exhaled notes followed by two inhaled notes, except for a few notes at the high end.

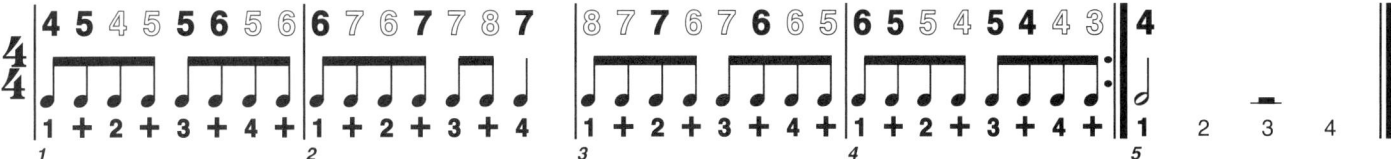

43. Botany Bay

The notes of this traditional Australian song all come from the C major scale. If you listen to the recording, you will hear the guitar playing chords as an accompaniment. These chords are all built on notes from the C major scale also.

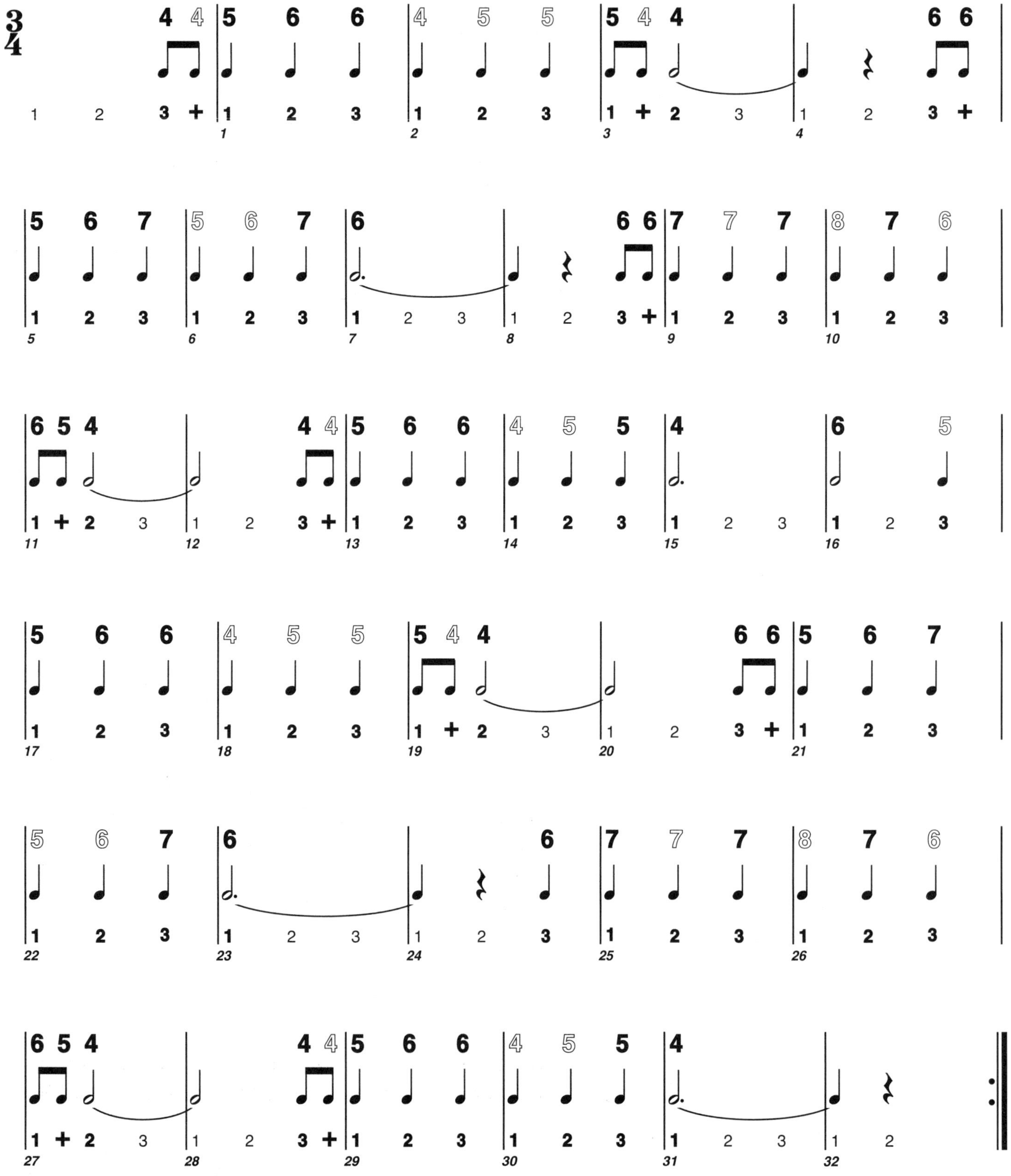

THE DOTTED QUARTER NOTE

 A dot written after a quarter note means that you hold the note for **one and a half beats**.

 A dotted quarter note is often followed by an eighth note.

Count 1 2 +

 44.

 45. Oh Susanna

This well known folk song makes use of the dotted quarter note followed by an eighth note.

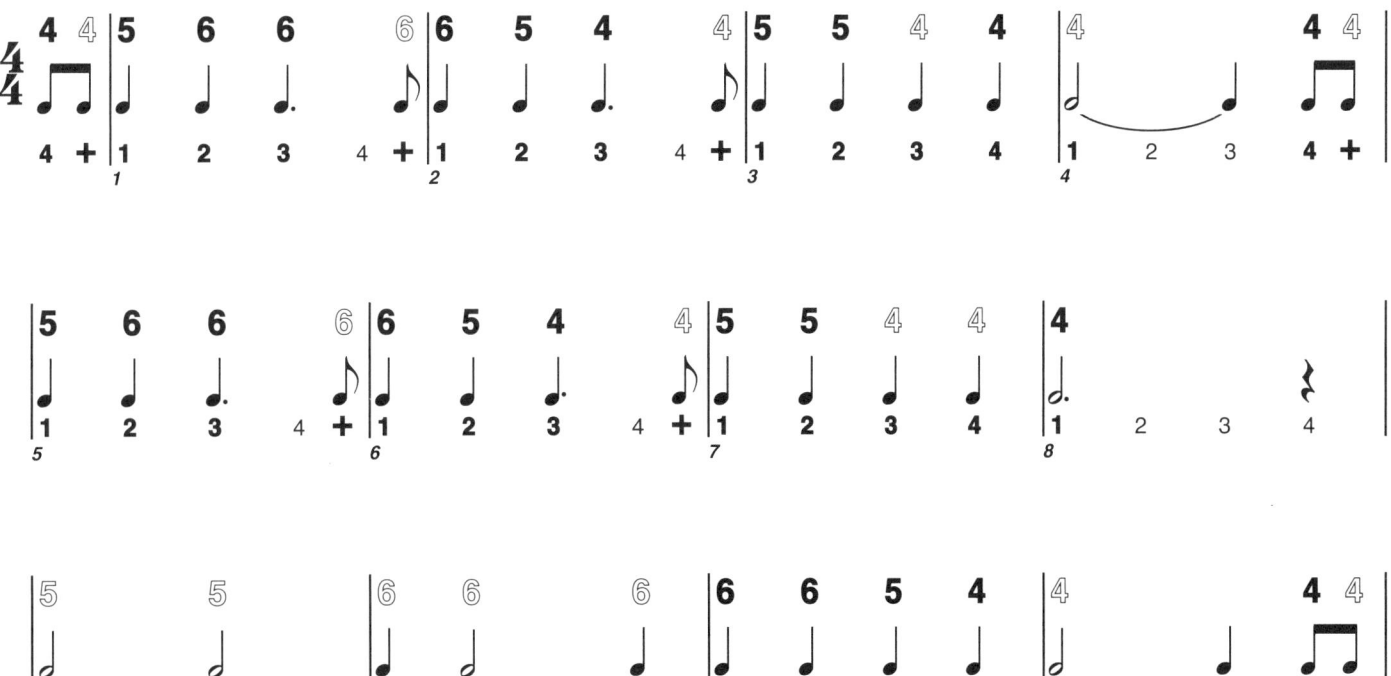

The following example demonstrates a different use of the dotted quarter note. This time an eighth note is followed by the dotted quarter. This creates an effect known as **syncopation** which means displacing the normal flow of accents from on the beat to off the beat. Syncopation will be dealt with in lesson 8. Syncopated rhythms can be difficult at first, so count and tap your foot as you play.

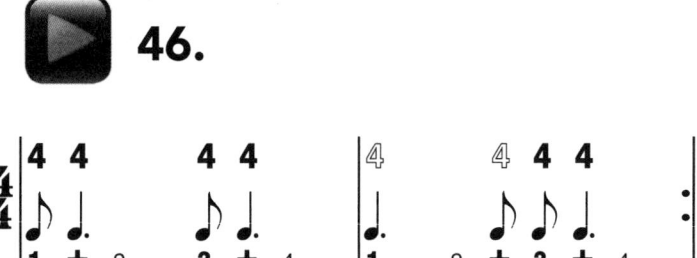

46.

47. Swing Low, Sweet Chariot

This song makes use of both of the dotted quarter note figures presented in this lesson. It is played at the very top end of the harmonica. Take it slowly at first and count as you play.

LESSON EIGHT

THE TRIPLET

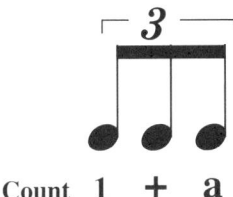

Count **1 + a**

An eighth note **triplet** is a group of **three** evenly spaced notes played within one beat. Triplets are indicated by three eighth notes grouped together by a bracket (or a curved line) and the numeral **3**. The eighth note triplets are played with one third of a beat each. Triplets are easy to understand once you have heard them played. Listen to the following example on the recording to hear the effect of triplets.

 48. How to Count Triplets

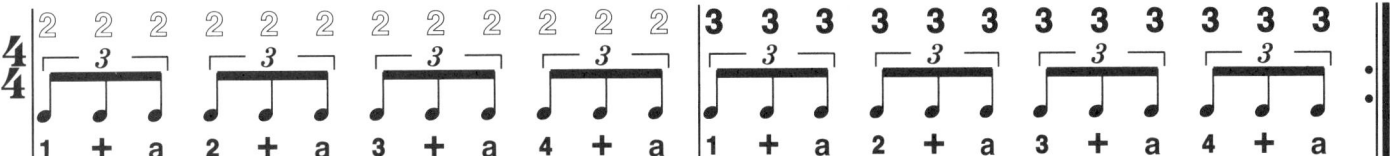

 **49.**

Here is a triplet variation on the Blues riff you learnt in lesson 6. This one is played **cross harp in the key of G**.

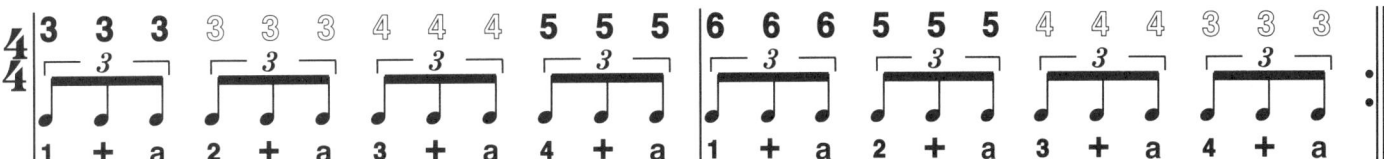

 50.

This one is a Blues intro riff also played cross harp in the key of G. Listen to how effectively this triplet rhythm works with the other instruments.

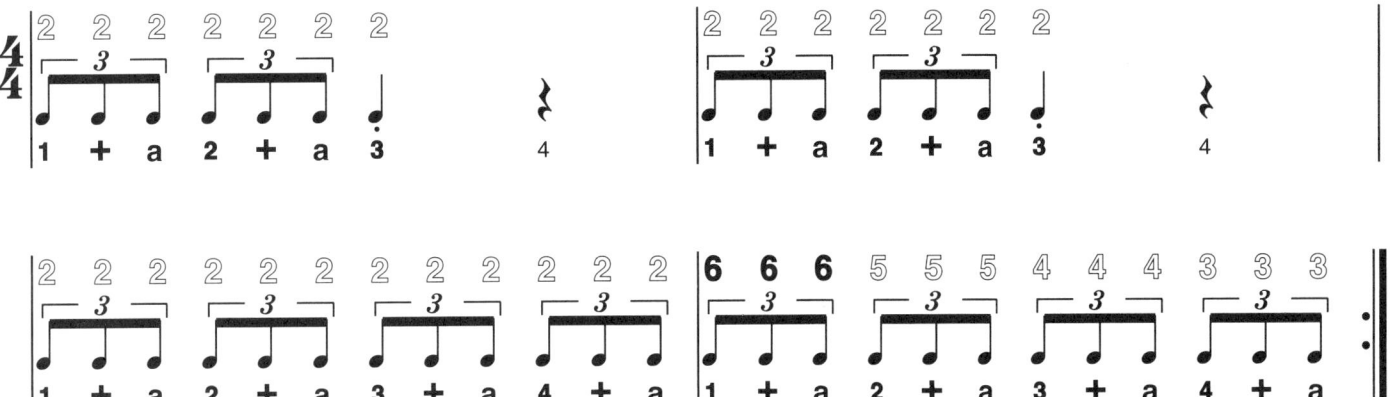

SWING RHYTHMS

A **swing rhythm** can be created by playing only the first and third notes of a triplet. Play the following example which contains a triplet on the second beat.

 51.

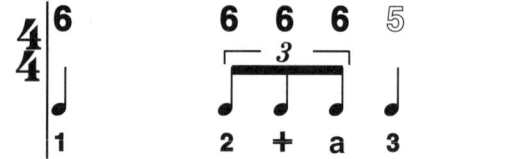

This example has the first and second notes of the triplet group tied. This gives the example a swing feel.

 **52.**

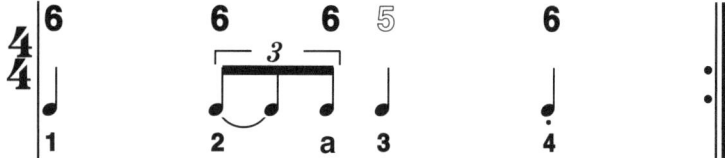

The two eighth note triplets tied together in the previous example can be replaced by a quarter note.

53.

To simplify notation, it is common to replace the ♩ ♪ with ♪♪ , and to write at the start of the piece ♪♪ = ♩ ♪ as illustrated below in example 54.

 **54.**

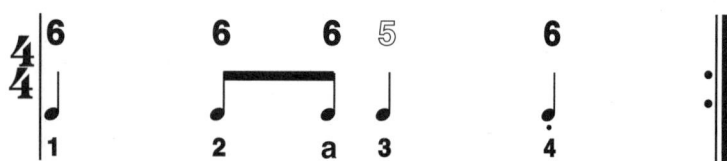

THE SHUFFLE

By using a constant stream of swinging eighth notes, an effect known as the **shuffle** is produced. The following example contains the now familiar cross harp Blues riff played as a shuffle.

 55.

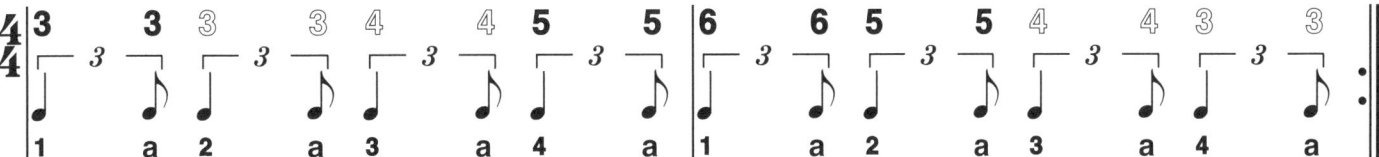

 56.

Here is the same riff extended to a full 12 bar Blues progression.

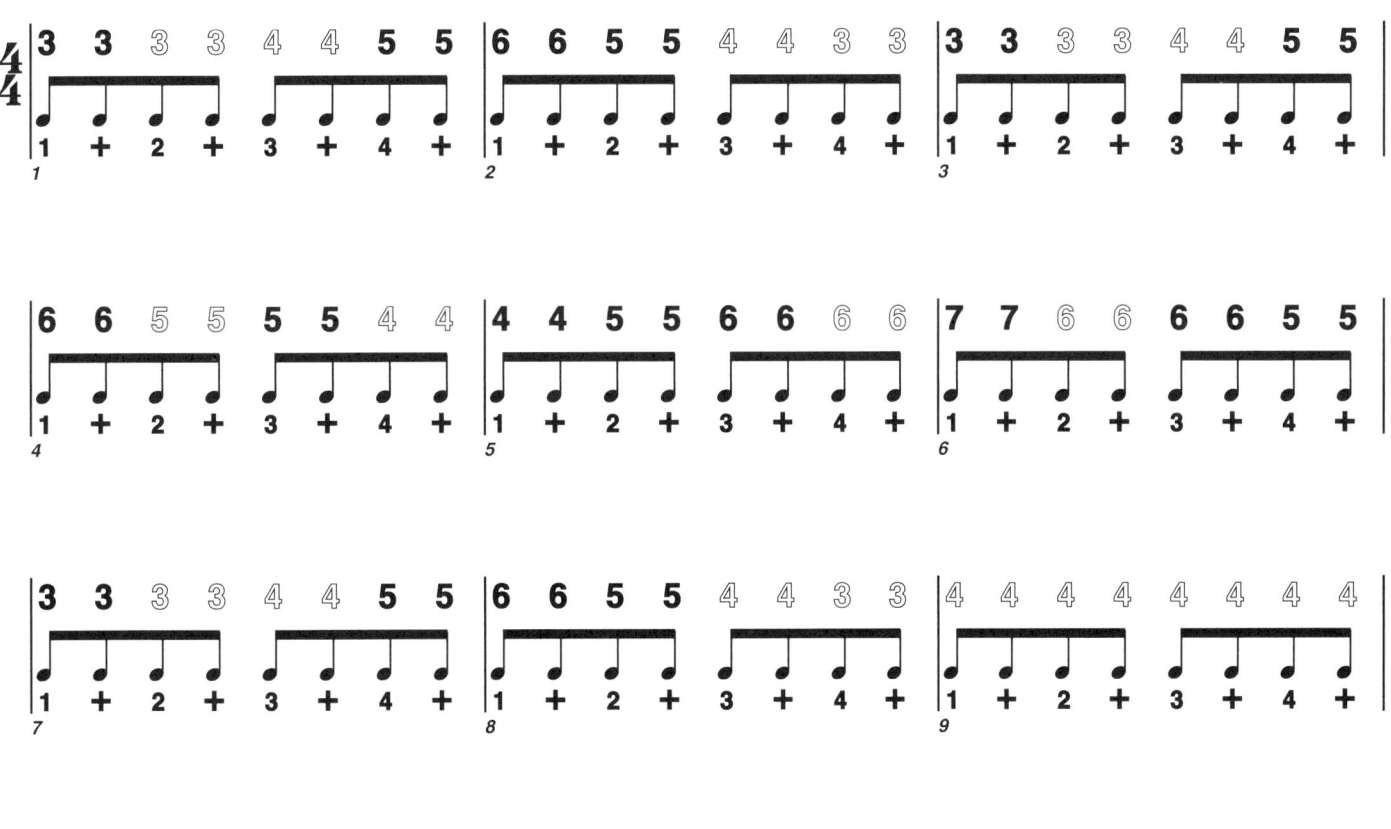

57. Battle Hymn of the Republic

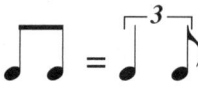

Here is another song played with a shuffle feel. This one is in the key of C.

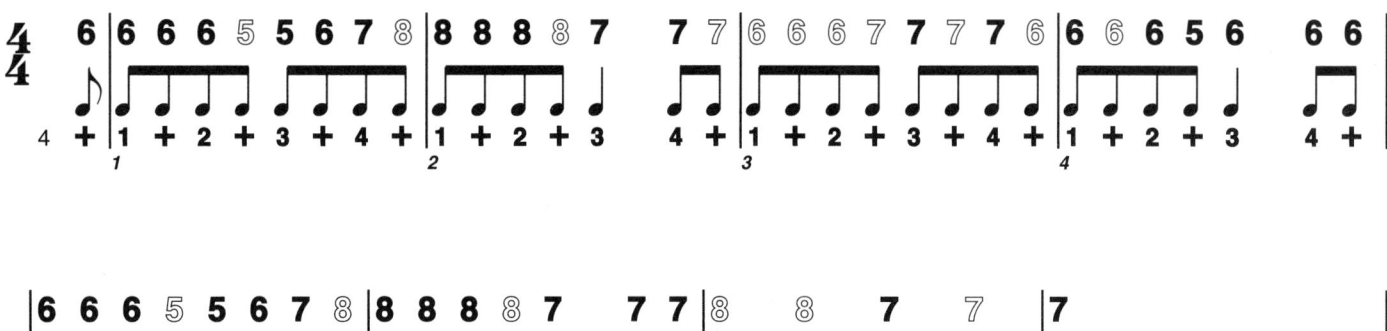

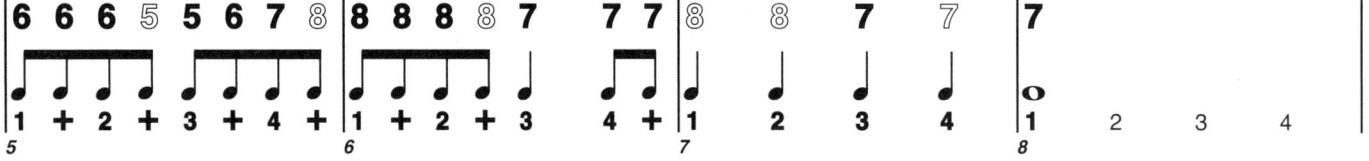

SYNCOPATION

As mentioned in the previous lesson syncopation means displacing the normal flow of accents in the music, usually from on the beat to off the beat. One of the most common ways of creating syncopated rhythms is to use rests on the beat as shown in the following example.

58.

 **59.**

Another common method of creating syncopated rhythms is to use ties as shown here.

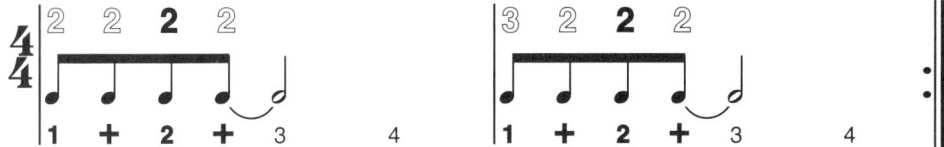 **60. Jamaica Farewell**

This well known Carribbean song contains many syncopated rhythms created by the use of both rests and ties. If you have trouble with syncopated rhythms, play them on one note first and count as you play.

LESSON NINE

SLIDING BETWEEN NOTES

Another common harmonica technique is to slide up or down to a specific note. This can really add drama and excitement to your playing. The symbol for a slide is a letter **S** above the note to which you are sliding, as shown here. Listen to the following example on the recording to hear the effect created by the use of slides.

 **61.**

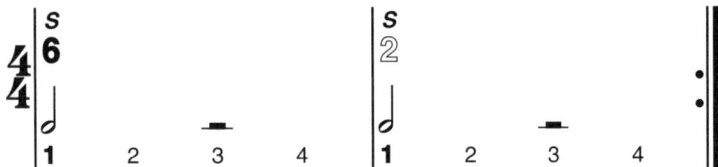

There is another effect called a trail off which is the reverse of the slide. A trail off is achieved by playing a note and then sliding away to an indefinite pitch. A trail off is indicated by a letter **T** above the note to which it applies, as shown in the following example.

 **62.**

63.

Here is a simple 12 bar Blues in the key of G demonstrating both slides and trail offs. Experiment with these techniques on other tunes you have learnt.

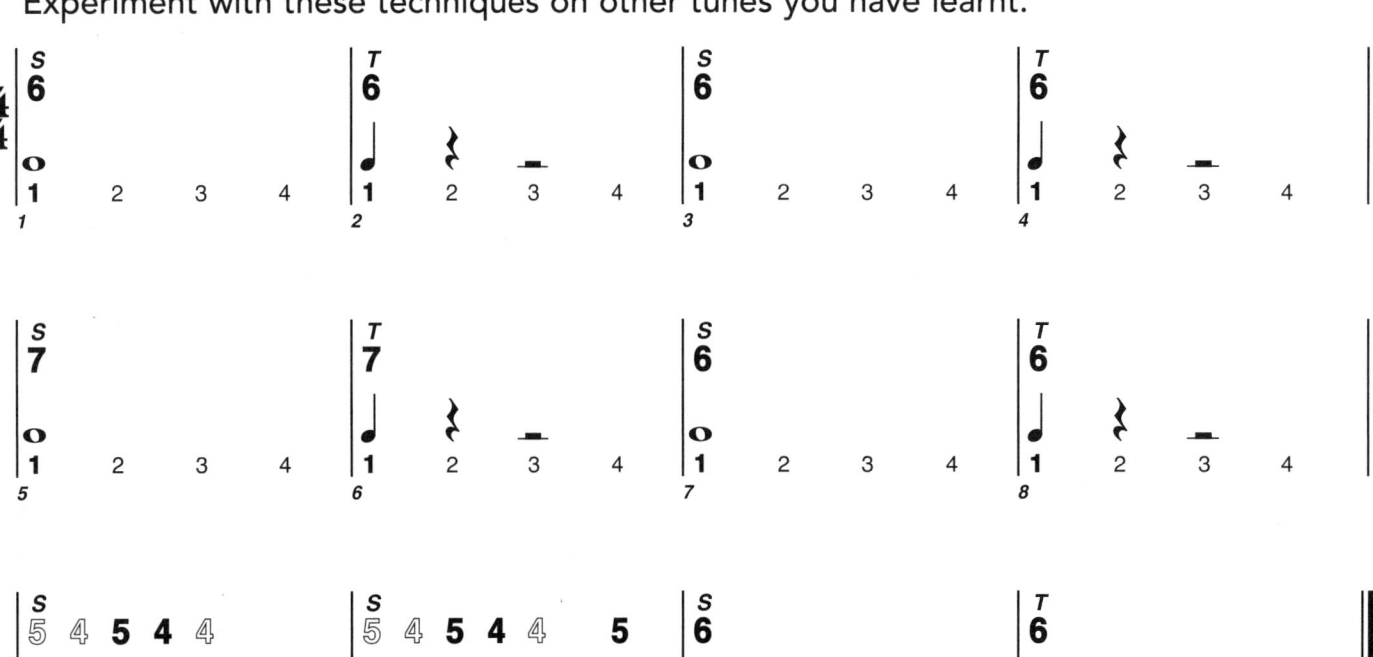

BENDING NOTES

One of the most exciting sounds in harmonica playing is the use of note bending. This technique can be difficult at first and may take several months to gain control of, but is essential for Blues playing, so it is definitely worth developing. The most common bends are the **inhale** notes on the low end of the harmonica, from 1 to 6. It is also possible to bend exhale notes on the high end of the harmonica. However, this is a more advanced technique and is not dealt with here. To bend a note, the **back of your tongue** (not the tip) needs to move **up and back** to the back of your mouth. This changes the flow of air, resulting in the note "bending" **downwards to a lower pitch**. A good way to get the right feel for the movement required for bending notes is to say the word **Yo**, or **Yaw**. Another useful exercise to prepare you for bending is to **whistle a descending major scale**. As you do this, notice how the back of your tongue moves back towards your throat as the pitch gets lower.

 64.

This example demonstrates a half step bend on the inhale note of hole 4, as indicated by the letter **B** above the note. Everyone has trouble with bending at first and many people can't do it at all when they begin, so be patient and keep at it. In time, your perseverence will definitely pay off.

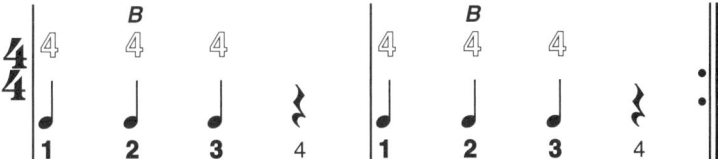

 65.

Here is an exercise to help you gain control of note bending. Listen carefully as you play and keep the notes even.

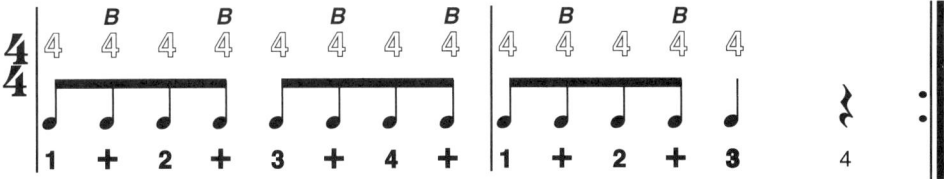

 66.

Now try this Blues lick which makes use of the note bend you have just learnt. A **lick** is a short musical phrase which can be used as a basis for improvisation or joined with other licks to form a solo.

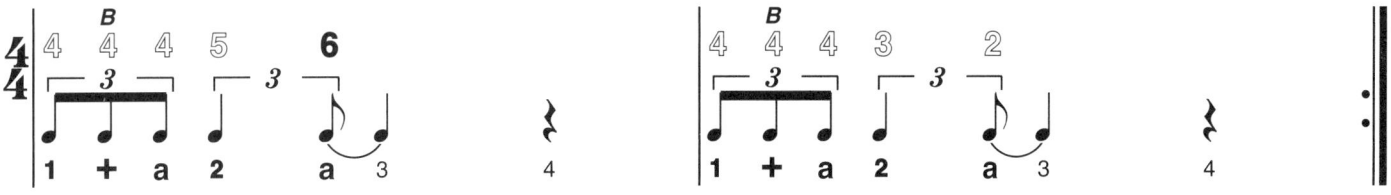

67.

Here are some more licks which make use of the note bend on 4. Try inventing some of your own.

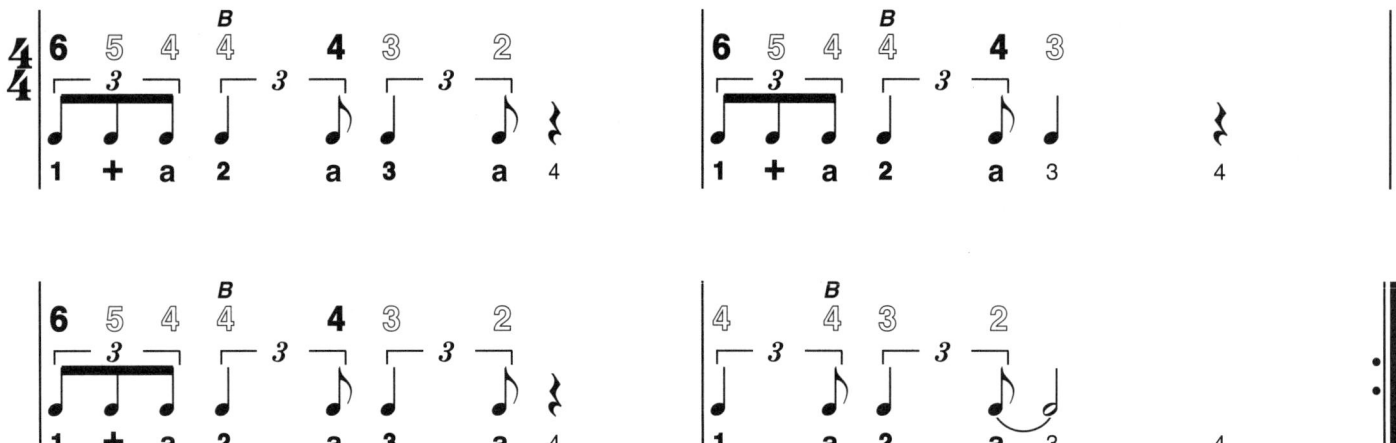

MORE NOTES TO BEND

Once you can bend the 4 note, try moving to holes 5 and 6 and bending these notes too. These are also half step bends and like the 4 bend, they may be difficult at first. The following example demonstrates these two bends.

68.

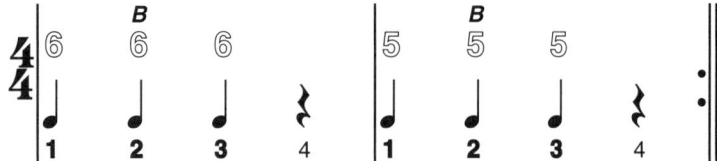

69.

Here is an exercise to help you gain control of all three of the bends you have learnt. Once again, listen carefully as you play and keep the notes even. If you are not sure of the notes you are bending to, listen to the example on the recording and then try to copy it.

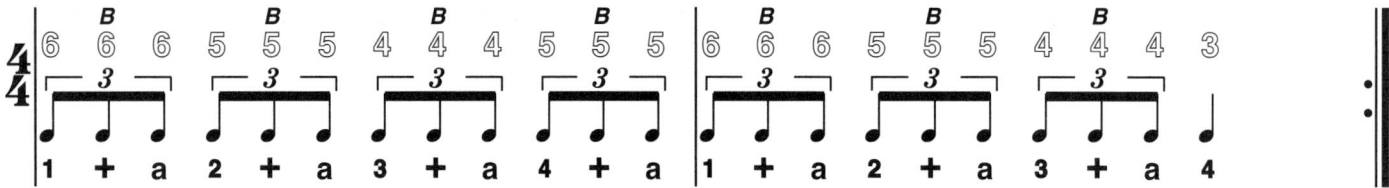

If you bend notes on hole 3, there are two possibilities instead of one. One of these is a **half step bend** and the other is a **whole step bend** which is a lower pitch than the first bend. A whole step bend is indicated by a line above the letter B ($\bar{B}$) The following example demonstrates both these bends.

 70.

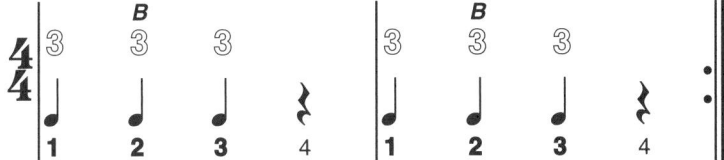

 71.

Here is a lick which makes use of both bends on hole 3 along with the bend on 4.

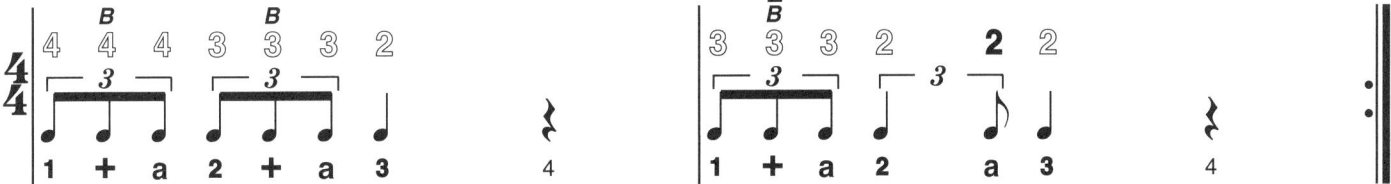

The next bend you will learn is another whole step bend, this time on hole 2. Like hole 3, there are two possible bends available here, but the half step bend is rarely used. Listen to the recording to hear the correct pitch to bend to.

 72.

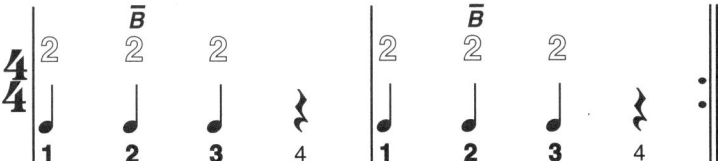

 73.

This exercise should help you gain control of the whole step bend on 2. This is one of the most difficult bends, so be patient with it and as with any other technique or lick you find difficult, practice it often but only for a short period each time.

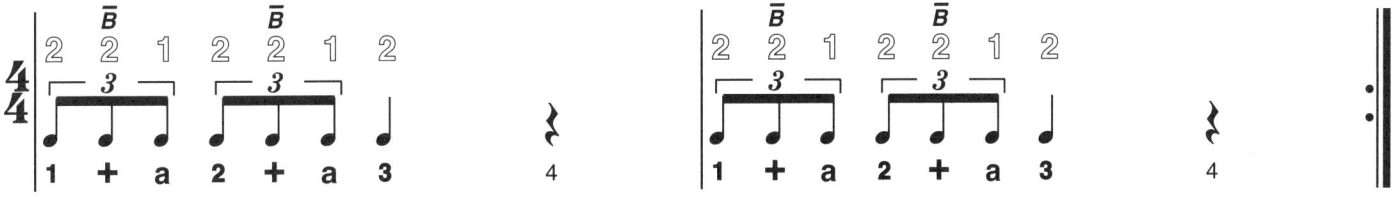

 **74.**

This riff makes use of the 2 bend, but this time you will need to land directly on the bent note instead of hearing the natural 2 pitch first. This may take some time to master, but produces a great sound so keep at it. This riff uses a common Blues technique known as **call and response**, which as a question and answer style of playing either between two instruments or an instrument and vocal.

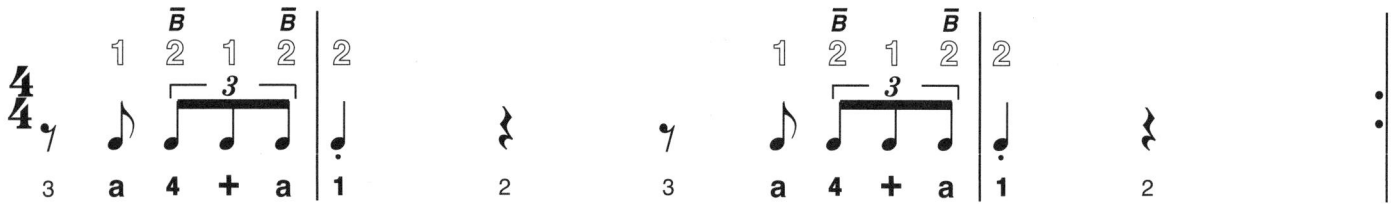

 **75.**

Here is a common variation on the previous riff, this time using the half step bend on hole 3.

GRACE NOTES

Sometimes, instead of holding a note for its full value, you can start on a note (e.g. a bent note) and immediately move to another note. These very quick notes are called grace notes. Bent grace notes can be thought of as a **wah** sound produced by the mouth. The "w" is the grace note and the "ah" is the following note held for its usual length of time. Bent grace notes are indicated in the notation by the letter **W** above the note to which it applies.

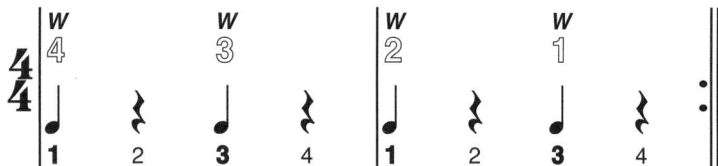 **76.**

 **77.**

Here is a lick making use of grace notes. This one also contains a slide, which is actually another method of producing grace notes.

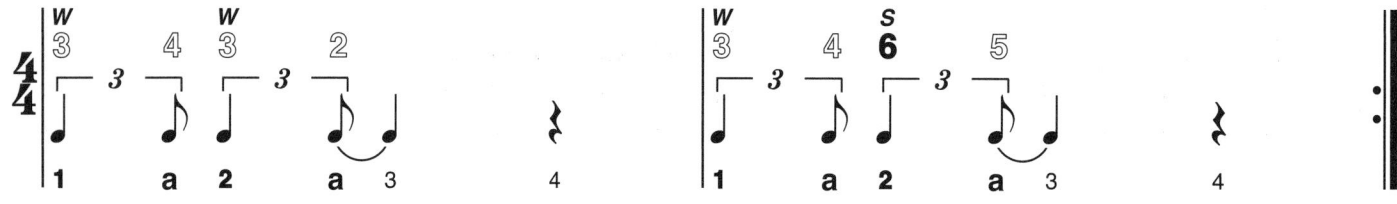

78.

Here is another lick containing both slide and bending grace notes.

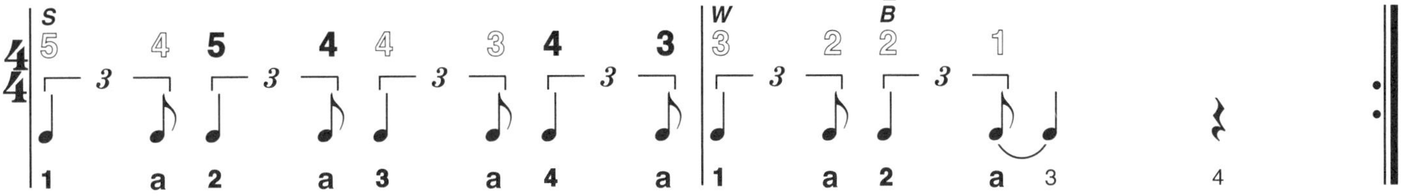

79. Bending the Blues

This 12 bar Blues in the key of G sums up all of the techniques presented in the lesson. It also contains double stops (2 notes played together). Listen to the recording and try to copy all the sounds you hear. Then try to memorize the solo one lick at a time. A great way to memorise something is to learn to sing it. First, listen to the recording many times and try to imitate the harmonica part using sounds close to the ones made by the harmonica (**wah**, **ta**, etc). Then try singing the harmonica part without the recording. Once you can sing something, you have it well in your memory and should find it a lot easier to play.

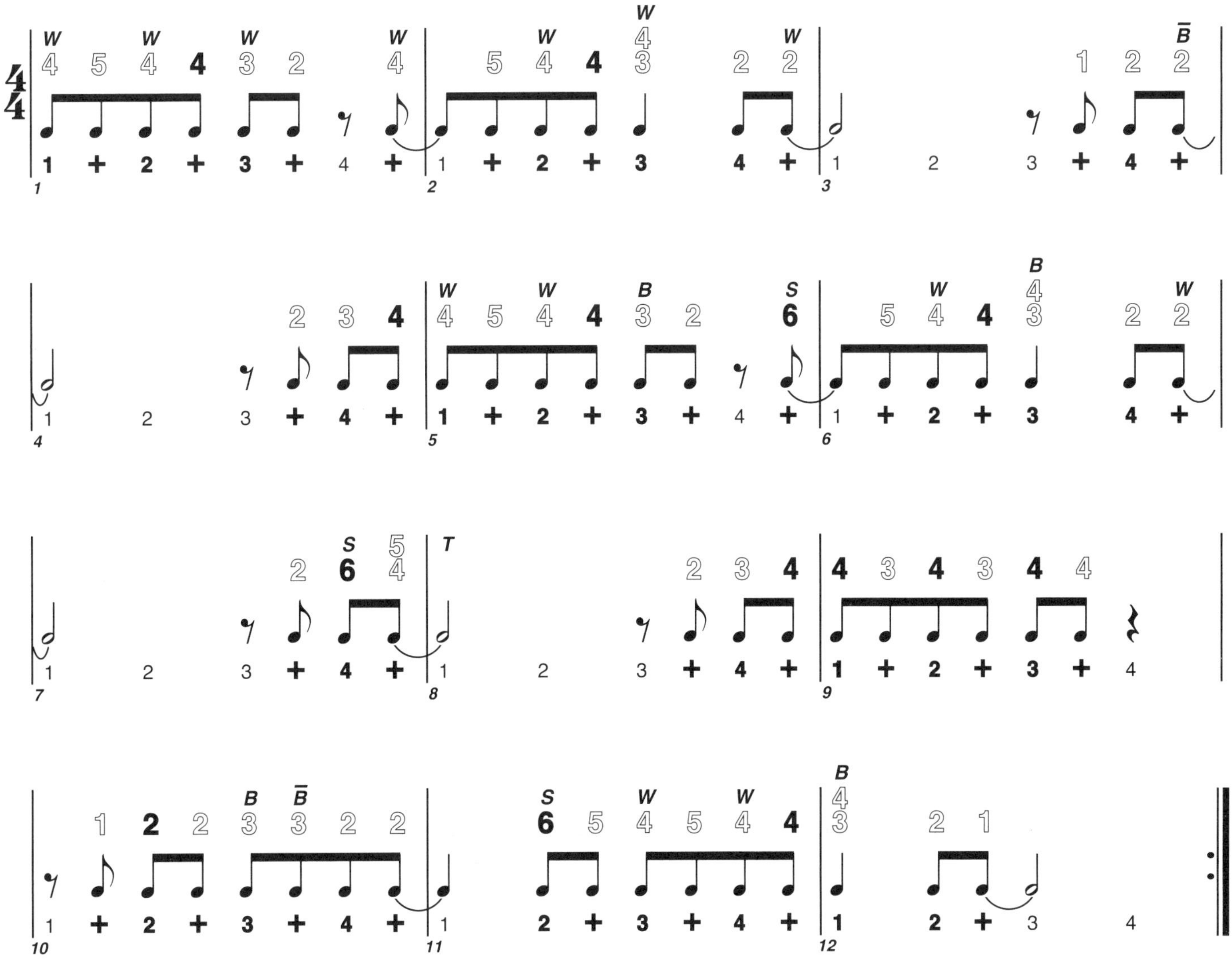

LESSON TEN

SIXTEENTH NOTES

 This is a **sixteenth note**.
It lasts for **one quarter** of a beat.
There are **four** sixteenth notes in one beat.
There are **16** sixteenth notes in one bar of
4/4 time.

Four sixteenth notes joined together.

Count   1   e   +   a

Say   one 'ee' and 'ah'

 ### 80. How to Count Sixteenth Notes

Tap your foot on each beat and count mentally as you play.

 ### 81.

Now try this example which contains sixteenth notes moving between two different notes.

 ### 82.

This one uses 16th notes moving between three different notes

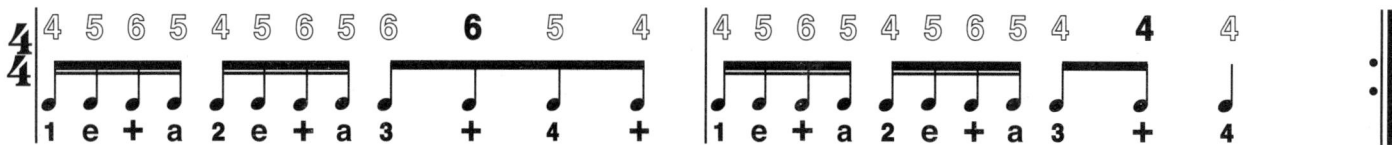

83.

Often in songs you will find two sixteenth notes grouped together with an eighth note as demonstrated in this example.

 84. Arkansas Traveler

This well known American folk song is in the key of C and contains many sixteenth notes as well as the combined eighth and sixteenth figures presented in the previous example. Take it very slowly at first and only increase the tempo (speed) when you can confidently play all the notes cleanly and evenly.

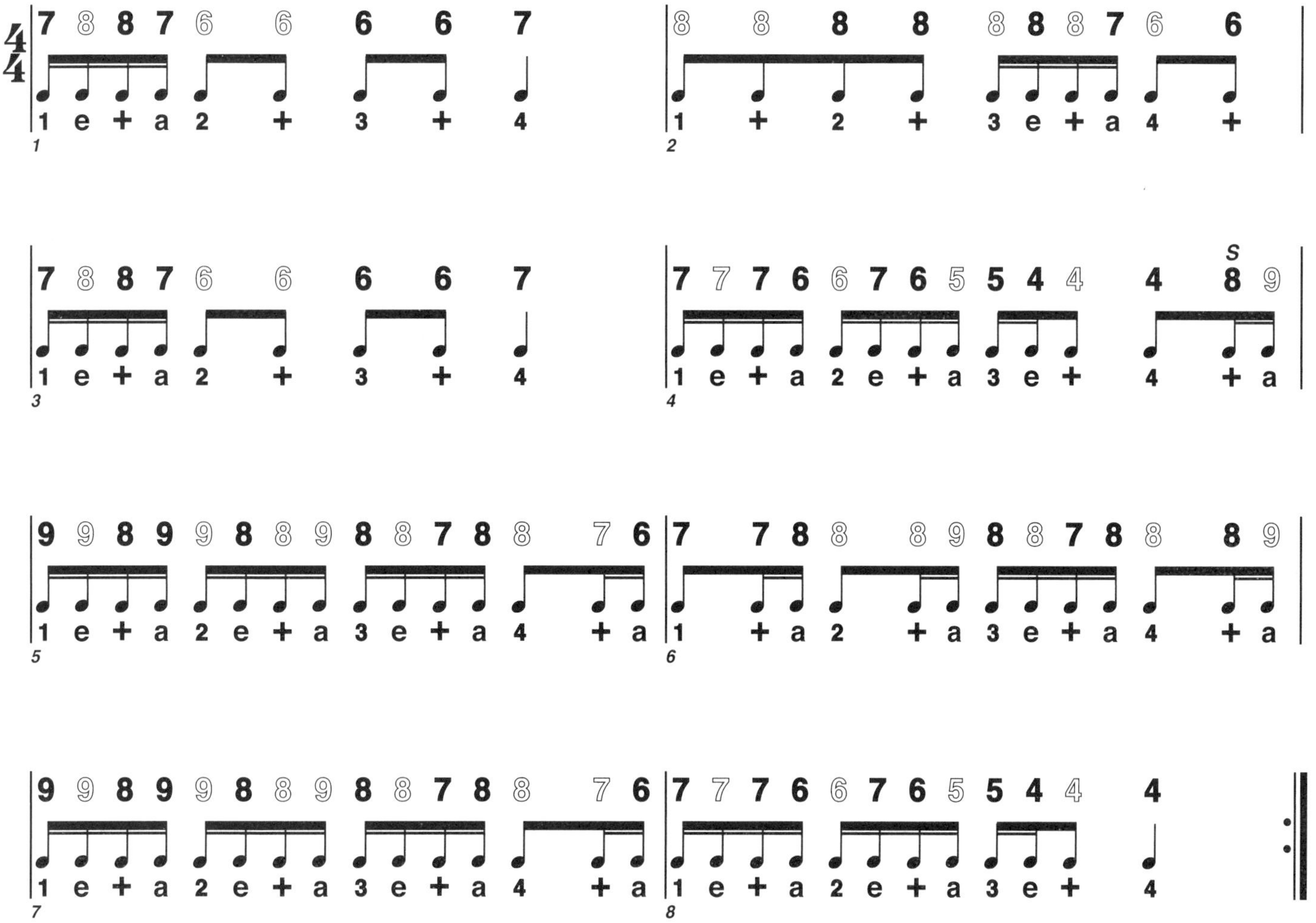

85. Cross Country

This Country flavored cross harp solo is a real challenge. It contains many sixteenth notes along with bends and grace notes using bends and slides. Listen to the recording and learn it one lick at a time if you have trouble with it.

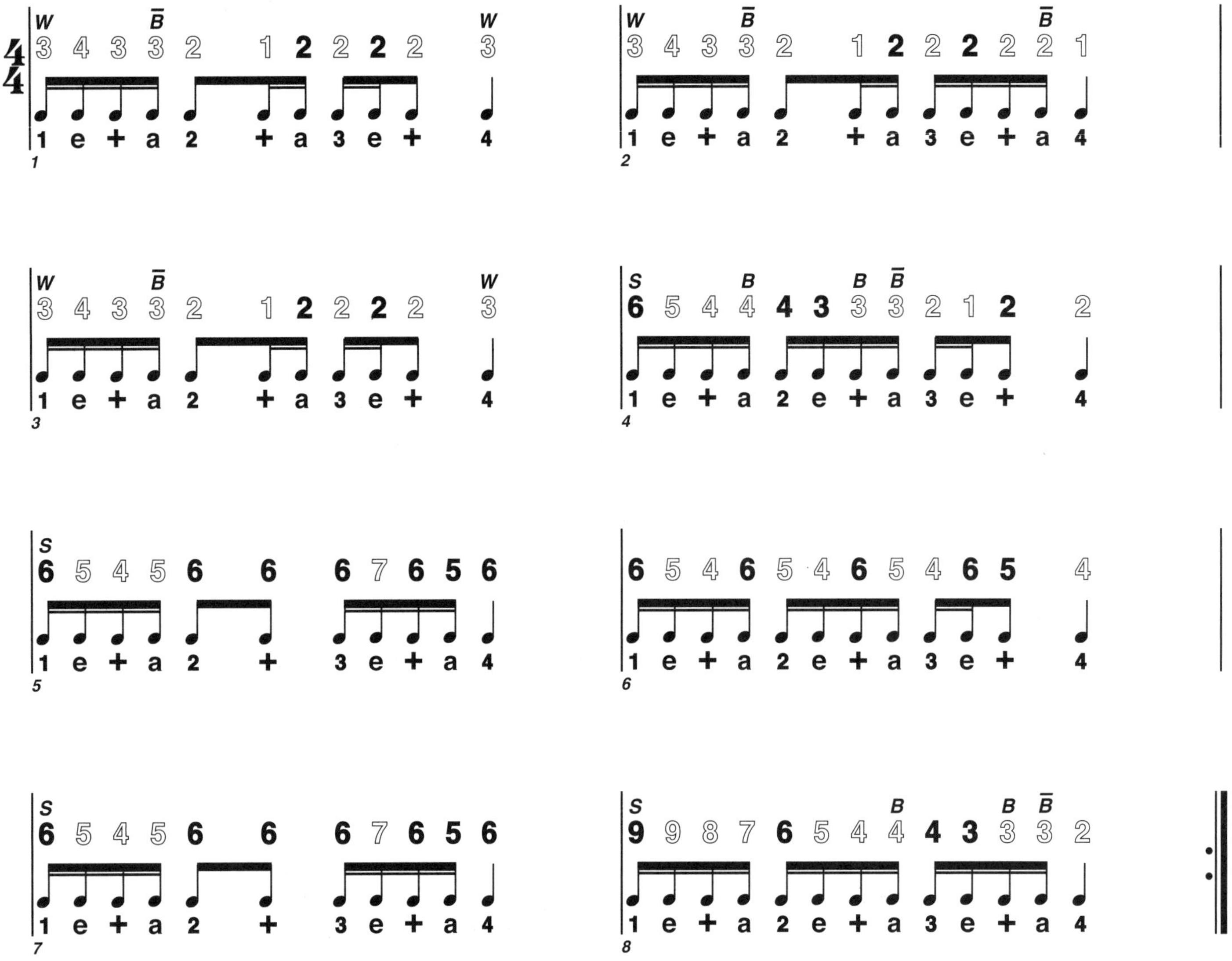

Measure 1: W 3 4 3 3 2 1 **2 2 2** 2 W 3 — counted 1 e + a 2 + a 3 e + 4

Measure 2: W 3 4 3 3 2 1 **2** 2 **2** 2 2 1 — counted 1 e + a 2 + a 3 e + a 4

Measure 3: W 3 4 3 3 2 1 **2 2 2** 2 W 3 — counted 1 e + a 2 + a 3 e + 4

Measure 4: S 6 5 4 4 **4 3** 3 3 2 1 **2** 2 — counted 1 e + a 2 e + a 3 e + 4

Measure 5: S 6 5 4 5 **6** **6** **6** 7 **6 5 6** — counted 1 e + a 2 + 3 e + a 4

Measure 6: 6 5 4 6 5 4 6 5 4 6 5 4 — counted 1 e + a 2 e + a 3 e + 4

Measure 7: S 6 5 4 5 **6** **6** **6** 7 **6 5 6** — counted 1 e + a 2 + 3 e + a 4

Measure 8: S 9 9 8 7 **6** 5 4 4 **4 3** 3 3 2 — counted 1 e + a 2 e + a 3 e + a 4

 ## 86.

Here is an example which moves between eighth notes, triplets and sixteenth notes. Tap your foot on each beat and count the subdivisions as you play.

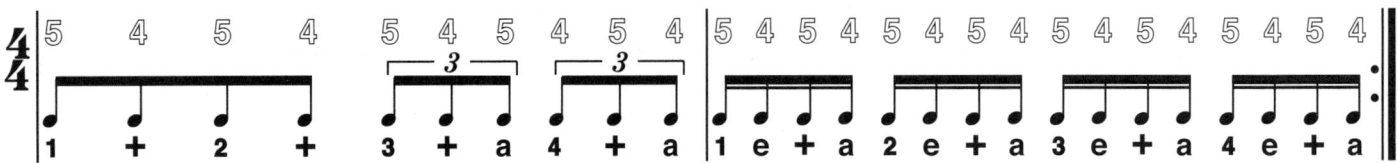

THE TRILL

Another exciting sound often played on the harmonica is the **trill**. A trill is a rapid alternation between two inhaled notes or two exhaled notes. This can be achieved either by rapidly moving the harmonica from side to side while maintaining a steady breath, or by rolling the head from side to side while holding the harmonica steady. Both these methods are common in harmonica playing. A trill is indicated by two holes (eg $\frac{5}{4}$) with the symbol *Tr* written above them.

 87.

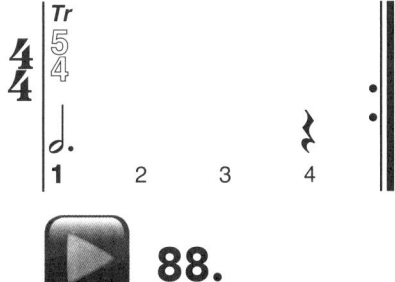

 **88.**

Here is a typical Blues lick using the trill on holes 4 and 5.

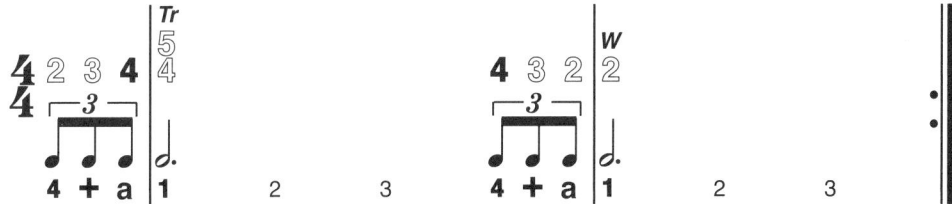

 **89.**

There is always more than one way to play something. This example contains exactly the same notes as the previous example except that the rhythm has been changed. Experiment with different rhythms for other licks you have learnt.

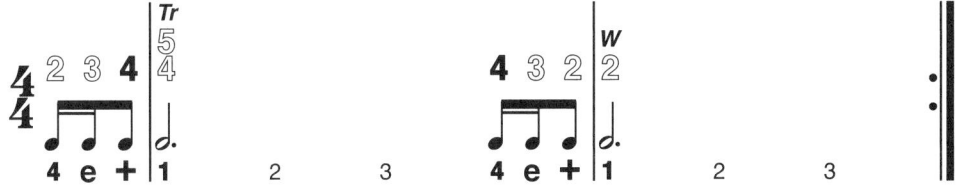

90.

Here is another variation. This time the rhythm is exactly the same as example 88 but the notes have been changed. The trill here is between holes 3 and 4.

91.

Here is one more lick featuring the trill. Try making up some of your own licks and adding trills to them.

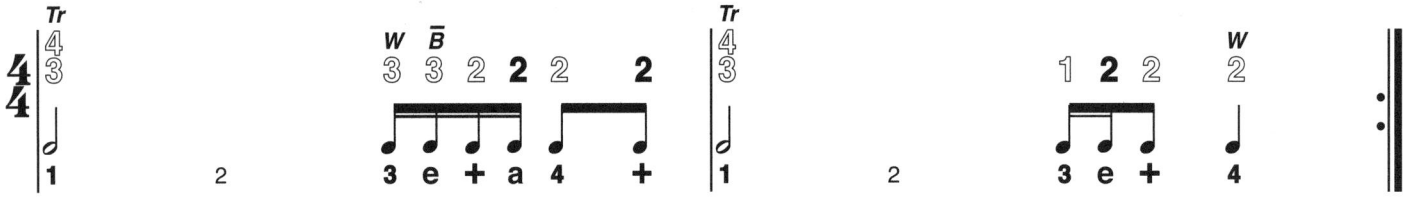

CALL AND RESPONSE

As mentioned in lesson 9, **call and response** is a typical Blues and Gospel technique where one instrument or voice answers another. In the following example, the harmonica does not play in the first two bars. On the recording, the vocalist sings in these two bars and then the harmonica answers in the following two bars. This format is then repeated for the rest of the 12 bar progression. Many Blues songs are played in this exact manner. Try singing a line and then answering your voice with the harmonica, or get a friend to sing and you answer with the harmonica.

 92. Come Back Darlin'

LESSON ELEVEN

WHAT ARE ALL THESE SOUNDS?

Through the course of the book you have learnt many different notes in two different playing positions (first position and second position or cross harp). There are various musical ways of describing all these notes and relating them to keys. This is the main subject of lesson 11. There are two different ways to approach this final lesson. You may wish to study each scale and description in detail, or you may wish to use it basically as a reference while continuing to develop your playing by ear and asking questions of other musicians. There are many good harmonica players who have very little knowledge of music theory. However, it is the author's belief that you can get a lot further if you understand the sounds you are making and how to transfer them to harmonicas in other keys.

NOTES ON THE C HARMONICA

The following diagram shows the names of all of the notes you have learnt in the book. There are technically a few more possible notes you could find on the C harmonica, particularly by bending the higher exhale notes, but these have been omitted to keep the diagram as simple as possible. The symbol ♭ beside some of the notes is a **flat sign**. Flat means a lower pitch. By using these signs it is possible to indicate pitches halfway between letter names, e.g. the note D♭ is halfway between the notes C and D.

Exhale	C	E	G	C	E	G	C	E	G	C
	1	2	3	4	5	6	7	8	9	10
Inhale	D	G	B	D	F	A	B	D	F	A
Bend	D♭	F	B♭ or A	D♭	E	A♭				

If you wish to study harmonica playing seriously, it is worth taking some time to memorize the names of the notes on the harmonica along with their **scale degrees** which measure the distance of each note from the key note (in this case, **C**). The **key** is the central note which all the other notes relate to. Since there are seven different notes in the major scale, each note can be given a number from 1 to 7 as shown below. When the number 8 is reached, the pattern begins again, since 8 is a repeat of 1 an octave higher.

Note Name	C	D	E	F	G	A	B	C
Scale Degree	1	2	3	4	5	6	7	8

Once you know how to bend notes, it is possible to play a lower octave of the C major scale starting on hole **1**. This example demonstrates the low octave without bends and then the full scale with bends.

 **93.**

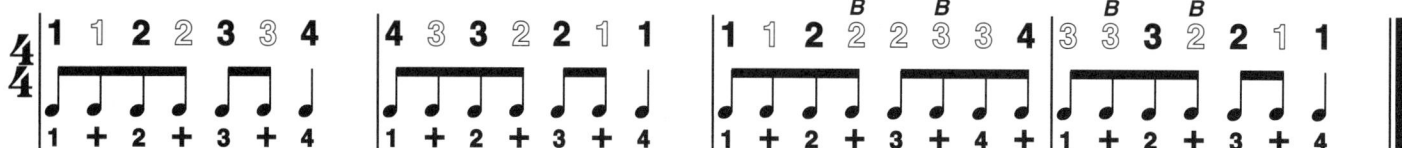

 94. Two Octave C Major Scale

Once you have control of the low octave of C major, add it to the middle octave which you already know.

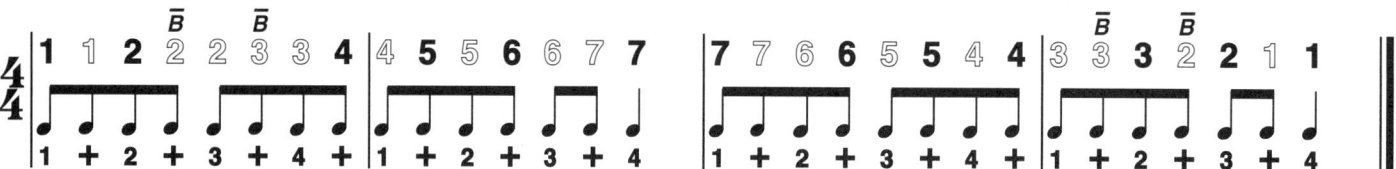

If you try playing the highest octave of the C major scale starting on **7**, you will find that the note **B** (the **7th** degree) is missing, so you get C (1), D (2), E (3), F (4), G (5), A (6) and C (8). The following example contains three octaves of the C major scale (apart from the missing B note), which is the complete range of the C harmonica. **All** ten hole diatonic harmonicas have a range of 3 octaves regardless of what key they are tuned to.

 95. The Complete Range of the C Harmonica

As you play this example, try to mentally name the notes as you play. If you have trouble, think do, re, mi at first, then name the notes. Once you can do this, play it again and mentally sing the scale degrees as you play. Remember that the octave of C (degree 8) is equal to degree 1, so count each new C as a **1** rather than an **8**. E.g. **1,2,3,4,5,6,7,1,2,3,4,5,6,7,1,2,3**, etc. It is important to remember that scale degrees are purely theoretical numbers which relate to all instruments regardless of their playing techniques. Do not confuse scale degrees with the numbers of the holes on the harmonica.

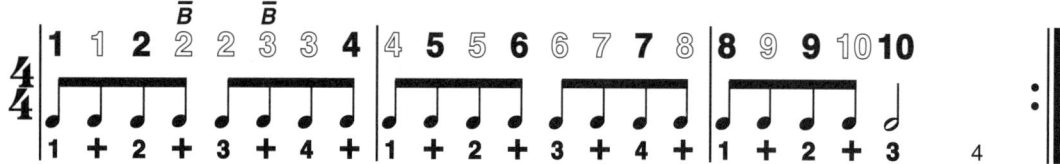

THE MAJOR PENTATONIC SCALE

You will have noticed that in order to play the low octave of the C major scale, it was necessary to produce some extra notes by bending. Also, in the high octave, the note **B** was missing. This is because of the way the harmonica is tuned. It is possible to create melodies without all of the notes of the major scale. In fact, the major scale is only one of many different scales used in music. By leaving out the **4th** and **7th** degrees of the major scale, the major pentatonic scale is created. As the name suggests, pentatonic scales contain only five different notes. There are many melodies, particularly in folk and gospel music which are derived from the major pentatonic scale. One you have already learnt is *Swing Low, Sweet Chariot*. Others include *Amazing Grace* and *Tom Dooley*. The C major pentatonic scale is shown below.

C Major Pentatonic

C	D	E	G	A	C
1	2	3	5	6	8(1)

 96.

Here is the C major pentatonic scale played in the middle octave. Once again, try mentally naming the scale degrees as you play.

 97.

Once you are comfortable playing the major pentatonic scale in the middle octave, try playing it over the full 3 octave range of the harmonica. As with the C major scale, you will need to bend hole 3 to obtain the **6th** degree of the scale (an **A** note) in the low octave.

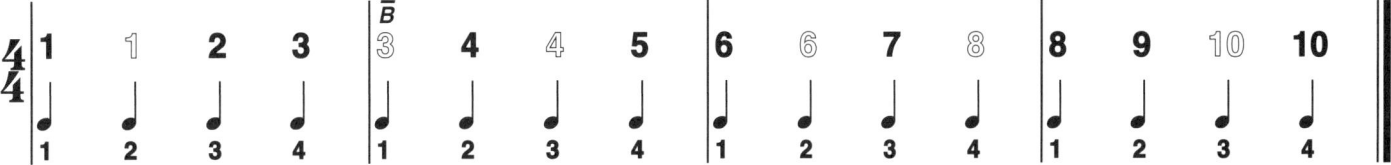

LESSON TWELVE

CROSS HARP SOUNDS

When you play cross harp, you are playing in the key of **G**. This means that all the scale degrees for cross harp playing relate to the note G instead of C. To play the G major scale, the note **F sharp** is required. Just as a flat lowers the pitch of a note, a sharp (♯) raises the pitch of a note. This means that the note **F♯** is halfway between F and G. The note F♯ is not available on the C harmonica, which means the G major scale cannot be played on the C harmonica. However, the cross harp position is normally used for more bluesy sounds which do not use the major scale but do contain a **flattened 7th** degree. By flattening the 7th degree of the major scale, the **mixolydian** scale or mode is produced. A comparison of the G major scale and the G mixolydian scale is shown below.

G Major Scale

G	A	B	C	D	E	F♯	G
1	2	3	4	5	6	7	8

G Mixolydian Scale

G	A	B	C	D	E	F	G
1	2	3	4	5	6	♭7	8

 98.

Here is the G mixolydian scale played first in the middle octave and then over two octaves. Notice the slightly mournful sound produced by the ♭**7** degree. This is one of the sounds that makes cross harp so effective for Blues playing. As you play this example, mentally name the scale degrees, remembering that G is the keynote instead of C. The note G can be found at holes 2, **3**, **6**, and **9**. The solo "**Cross Country**" which you learnt in lesson 10 uses the G mixolydian scale.

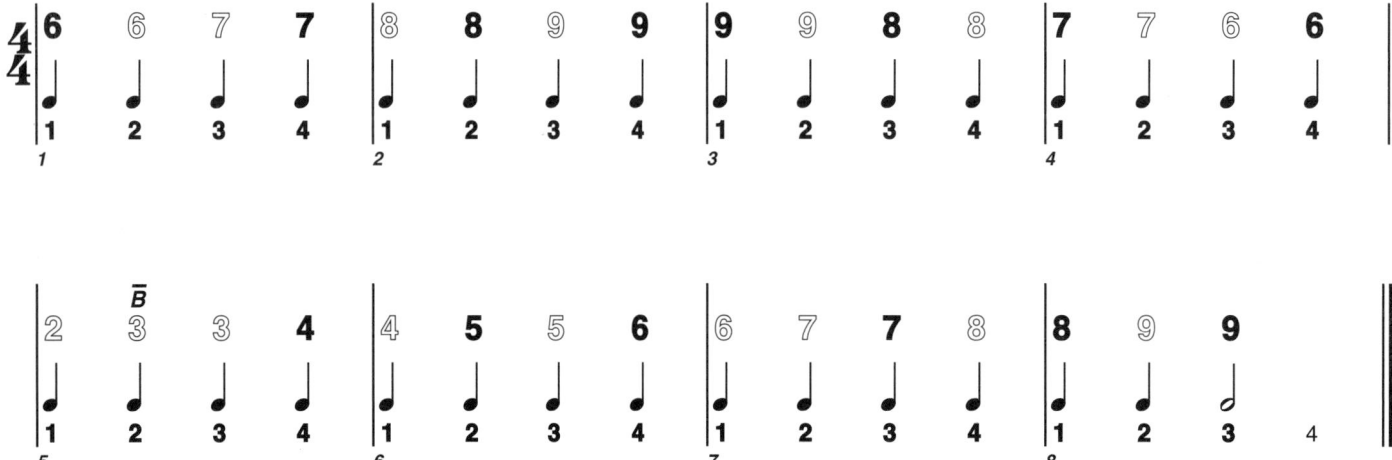

THE G MAJOR PENTATONIC SCALE

It is also possible to use the cross harp position to play the G major pentatonic. Remember that the major pentatonic scale is like a major scale with the 4th and 7th degrees omitted. Shown below is a comparison of the G mixolydian scale and the G major pentatonic scale.

G Mixolydian

G	A	B	C	D	E	F	G
1	2	3	4	5	6	♭7	8

G Major Pentatonic

G	A	B		D	E		G
1	2	3		5	6		8

 99.

Here is the G major pentatonic scale played over two octaves. Once again, mentally name the scale degrees as you play. Do this until you know which degree you are on as soon as you play it.

100. Amazing Grace

Here is the song Amazing Grace played cross harp in the key of G. All of the notes of this song come from the G major pentatonic scale. The bends from **B** to **A** on hole 3 can be tricky, so take care with them.

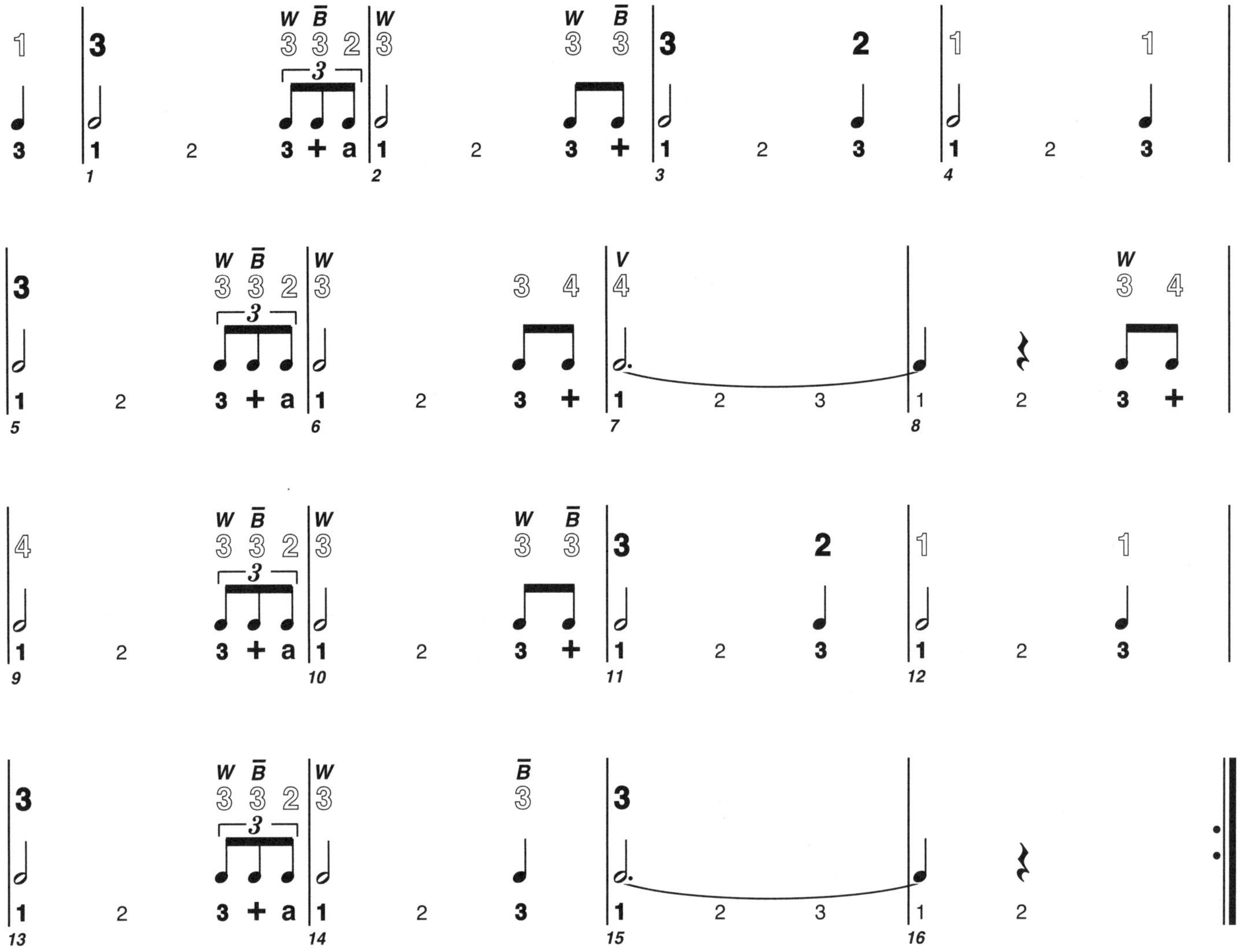

THE MINOR PENTATONIC SCALE

There are **two** different types of pentatonic scale, the major pentatonic and the **minor pentatonic** which is shown below. As well as the flattened 7th degree, the minor pentatonic also contains a **flattened 3rd** degree. The scale degrees of the minor pentatonic scale are **1**, ♭**3**, **4**, **5** and ♭**7**.

G Minor Pentatonic Scale

G		B♭	C	D		F	G
1		♭**3**	**4**	**5**		♭**7**	**8**

Because of the way the harmonica is tuned, it is only possible to play the cross harp minor pentatonic scale on the low end of the harmonica. The scale is shown in the following example starting on hole 2 and finishing on hole **6**, along with part of the scale on the very low notes down as far as the 4th degree (**C**). (For more on the minor pentatonic scale and its uses, see *Progressive Beginner Blues Harmonica*).

101.

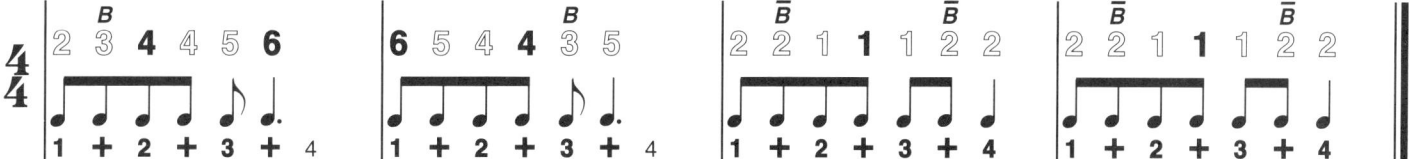

102.

Here is a riff you learnt in lesson 9 which is derived from the minor pentatonic scale. As you can hear, this scale is great for creating Blues sounds. It is also the most common scale used in Rock.

THE BLUES SCALE

By adding one extra note (the flattened fifth degree) to the minor pentatonic scale, the Blues scale is created. This scale is used by all instrumentalists to create Blues melodies.

G Blues Scale

G	Bb	C	Db	D	F	G
1	b3	4	b5	5	b7	8

103.

Like the minor pentatonic scale, the cross harp Blues scale can only be played on the low end of the harmonica. The G Blues scale is shown here along with a partial lower octave of the scale down as far as the 4th degree (C).

104.

Here is a lick derived from the G Blues scale. (For more information on the Blues scale and its uses, see *Progressive Beginner Blues Harmonica*).

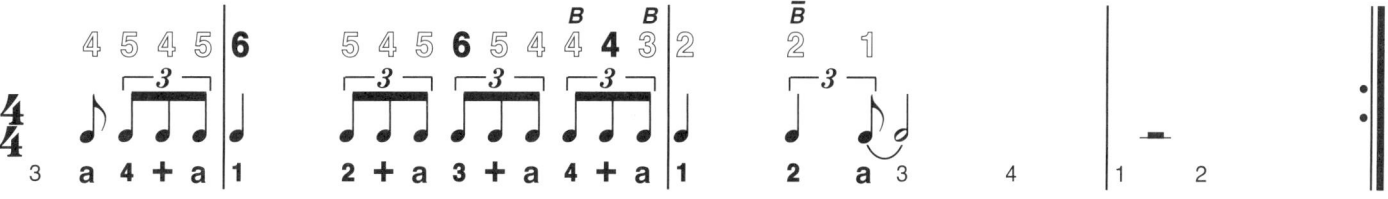

LESSON THIRTEEN

IMPROVISATION

Improvisation means creating your own melodies by ear. You now know more than enough to begin improvising. Although some licks and melodies are derived entirely from one scale, it is also common that notes from a combination of scales are used. Most musicians create new melodies totally by ear, drawing on all the sounds they are familiar with. When you are learning, the best approach is to learn all the sounds and scales but also to experiment with making up your own licks totally by ear. Composing is usually done by intuition based on subconscious knowledge and then rounded off with fine tuning based on conscious knowledge, i.e. the creating is done by ear and the theoretical analysis comes later.

A good way to start is to improvise with rhythm on one note only. Once you are comfortable doing this, try using the same rhythms and move between different notes. The following example demonstrates this technique.

 105.

This example uses a two bar rhythm played on the note G and then moved between three notes. If you are playing in the key of G and you improvise using the note G, you can't go wrong. If you are in the key of C, you could use the note C to begin with.

 **106.**

This one uses a repetition and variation approach which is a common improvising technique. One of the most important things to remember when using the repetition and variation technique is to keep your basic idea fairly simple. This makes it easy to develop and easy for the listener to follow what you are doing.

 ## 107. Wailin'

This final example is a Blues solo using many of the techniques you have learnt in the book. Listen to the recording to hear the expressions created by the use of each technique. As mentioned earlier, a good way to learn any new solo is to sing along with the recording to help get the sound in your memory. By now you should have a good grasp of the basics of harmonica playing. The best way to develop your playing further is to listen to your favourite albums and play along with them and also to begin playing with other musicians. Guitar and harmonica sound particularly good together, as do piano and harmonica. If you are serious about music it may also be worth taking some lessons, particularly in the area of understanding music. Having said that, the most important thing is to just **keep on playing!** If you like the Blues sounds presented in this book – bends, slides, trills, train rhythms etc, the book *Progressive Beginner Blues Harmonica* covers these subjects in more detail along with lots of other great Blues sounds.

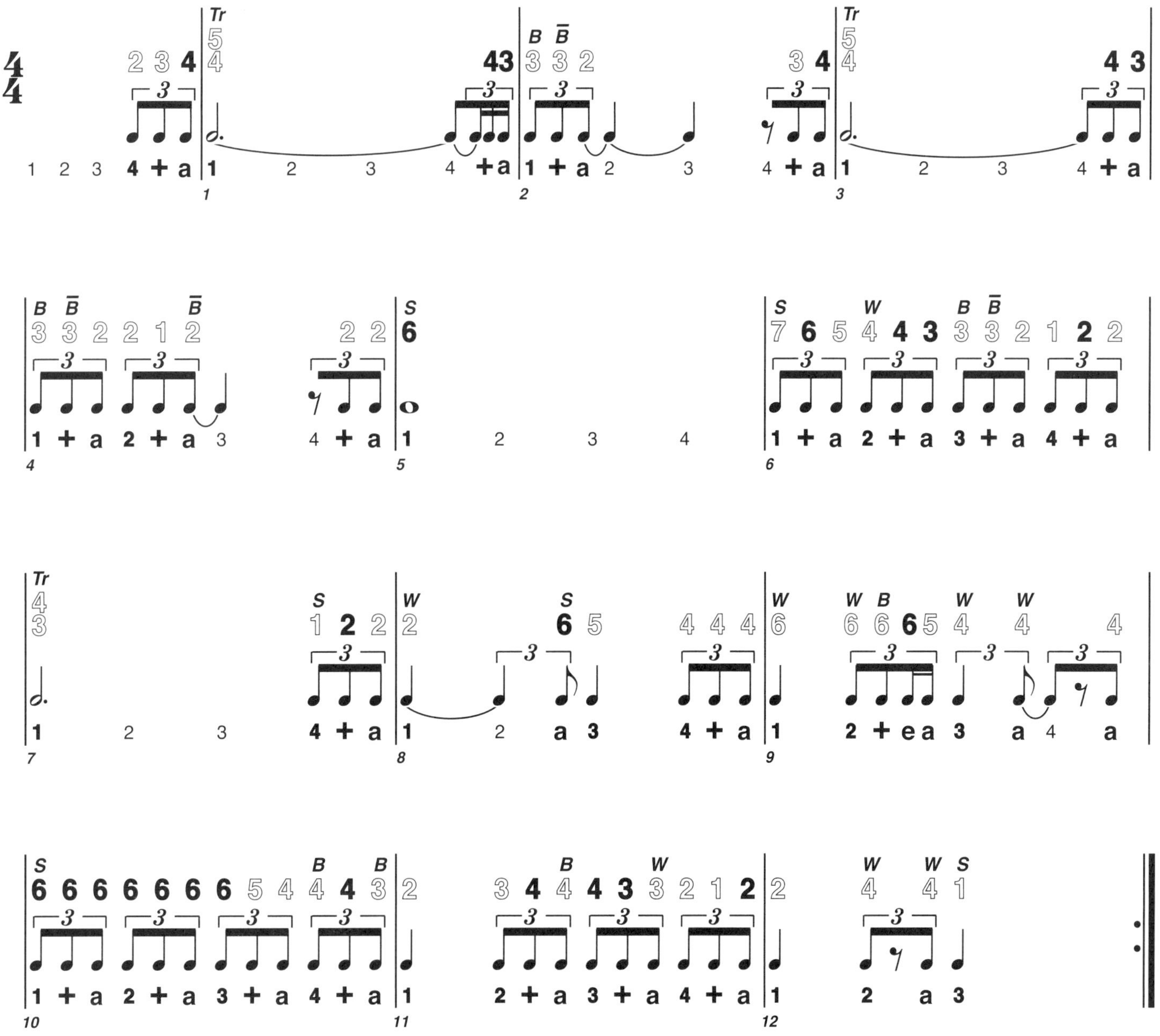

PLAYING IN OTHER KEYS

In this book you have learnt to play in two keys – C in first position and G in second position (cross harp). However, many times when you play with other musicans or play along with your favorite albums, other keys will be used. Once you are comfortable playing the C harmonica it is a good idea to get a few others in different keys. The playing techniques are identical regardless of the key you are playing in, only the actual pitch of the notes changes. This means that once you can play a song on the C harmonica, you can transfer it directly to any other harmonica and play the same holes with the same breathing and it will sound just as good. If you are playing an **A harmonica** in first position, you will be playing in the **key of A major**. If you are playing a **D harmonica** in first position, you will be playing in the **key of D major**. This means that if you are playing with a guitarist for example, you can easily find the correct key for many songs simply by choosing the harmonica with that key written on it.

For second position or cross harp playing however, it can sometimes be confusing trying to find the right harmonica to fit with what the other musicians are playing. In this situation it becomes more important to know the sounds on the harmonica as scale degrees. E.g. if a guitarist is playing a **Blues in E** (a common key for Blues), you would use an **A harmonica** to play cross harp in second position. The notes found at holes 2, **3**, **6** and **9** would all be **E notes on the A harmonica**. If you know that the notes at these holes are the first degree of any scale in the cross harp position, this makes it easier to understand why the A harmonica is the one chosen for a Blues in E. If you used any other key harmonica, the notes at these holes would not be E and the harmonica would not work for a Blues in E. There are actually more positions you can use on each harmonica, but these are more advanced and are not dealt with here. The following chart lists all the keys used in music along with the correct harmonica for playing second position cross harp with each key. The easiest way to check if you are using the right harmonica for the key is to play holes 2, **3**, or **6** and see if it is the same note as the key you want by testing it against a guitar or keyboard chord. If the guitar plays a **D chord**, your note should be a **D note**, if the guitar plays an **F chord**, your note should be an **F note**, etc. You can usually tell by ear if you have the correct note or not.

Cross Harp Chart

Guitar Key	Harmonica Key
C	F
G	C
D	G
A	D
E	A
B	E
F	B♭
D♭	G♭
A♭	D♭
E♭	A♭
B♭	E♭
F	B♭

UNDERSTANDING CHORDS

As mentioned in lesson 1, a chord is a group of 3 or more notes played simultaneously. Different types of chords can be formed by using different combinations of notes. The most common type of chord is the **major chord**. All major chords contain three notes, taken from the major scale of the same letter name. These three notes are the 1 (first), 3 (third) and 5 (fifth) degrees of the major scale, so the **chord formula** for the major chord is:

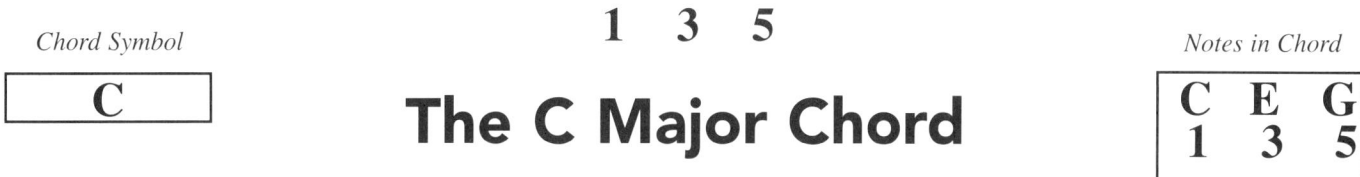

Chord Symbol

| C |

1   3   5

The C Major Chord

Notes in Chord

C	E	G
1	3	5

The C major chord is constructed from the C major scale. Using the above chord formula on the C major scale below, it can be seen that the C major chord contains the notes **C**, **E** and **G**.

C Major Scale

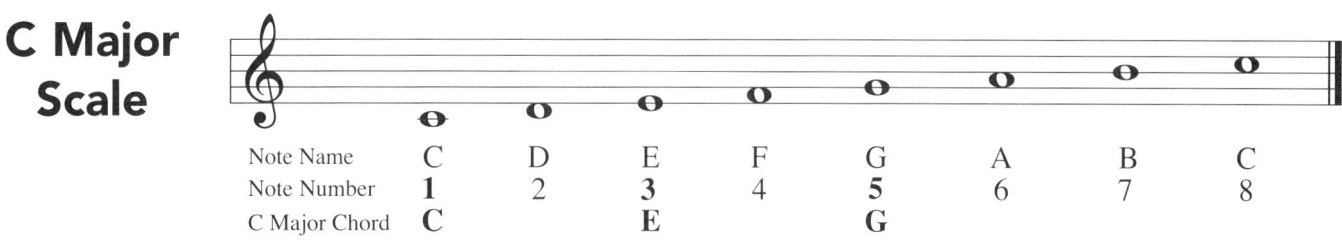

Note Name	C	D	E	F	G	A	B	C
Note Number	1	2	3	4	5	6	7	8
C Major Chord	C		E		G			

Once you have the correct notes for a C chord, you can double each of the notes as many times as you like. As long as the notes are still C, E and G, you still have a C chord. E.g. if you exhale through the harmonica and run your mouth from the bottom to the top of the instrument (holes 1 to 10) you produce a giant C chord covering three octaves, because **all** of the exhale notes on the C harmonica are either C, E or G.

Chords can be played more easily on some instruments than others. Two of the most common instruments used for chord playing are the guitar and the keyboard. Like the harmonica, it is possible to double (or even triple) the notes of a chord on these instruments. As long as you play the correct notes for any chord, they can be arranged in any order, e.g. a C chord could be played C E G, or E G C, or G C E, or even G E C. This is one of the reasons why chords may sound different when played on different instruments.

MELODY AND HARMONY

During the course of this book you have learnt to play songs using both chords and single notes. Any line played in single notes is called a **melody**. Any other accompanying notes such as chords are called **harmony**. There are many ways in which melody and harmony are used in music. One of the most common combinations is to have one instrument play the melody (e.g. harmonica) and another instrument play the harmony (e.g. guitar). When you play a song using chords on the harmonica, usually you are playing a combination of melody and harmony at the same time.

DIFFERENT TYPES OF CHORDS

Apart from starting a chord on the first degree of the scale, it is also possible to build chords on all the other notes of the major scale. A chord built on the second degree of the major scale would contain the 2nd, 4th and 6th notes of the scale. A chord built on the third degree of the scale would contain the 3rd, 5th and 7th notes of the scale, etc. The chord building pattern always consists of the root note (original note), the note two ahead of that note, and the note two ahead of that note, e.g. **C E G**, **D F A**, **E G B**, etc. If you build chords on the first, fourth and fifth degrees of the major scale, you end up with chords Ī, ĪV and V̄ which are the most common chords used for playing the Blues. Because of the pattern of tones and semitones in the major scale, not all the notes in these chords are comparatively the same distances apart. These different distances result in different types of chords such as minor chords and diminished chords. By adding more notes to the chords it is possible to create other chord types such as 7ths, 9ths and 13ths.

It is beyond the scope of this book to deal with all these chord types individually but if you are interested in how chords work, it is probably worth learning a bit of guitar or keyboard. This can also be beneficial in that you can quickly communicate with other musicians by understanding the terms they are using. Another major benefit of learning an instrument like guitar or keyboard is that you can accompany yourself. Many solo Blues and Folk performers use a harmonica rack worn around the neck in order to play guitar and harmonica at the same time. This method is great for your coordination and greatly increases your knowledge of the way notes and chords work together. Apart from this, it's a lot of fun and means you are not dependent on other people to make music with. To learn more about chords, chord progressions and keys, see *Progressive Blues Rhythm Guitar Method*, *Progressive Blues Keyboard Method* or *Progressive Rock Keyboard Method*. For easy reference for playing Blues in any key, here is a chart showing the basic chords Ī, ĪV and V̄ in all keys.

CHORDS Ī, ĪV AND V̄ IN ALL KEYS

KEY	Ī	ĪV	V̄	KEY	Ī	ĪV	V̄
C	C	F	G	F	F	B♭	C
G	G	C	D	B♭	B♭	E♭	F
D	D	G	A	E♭	E♭	A♭	B♭
A	A	D	E	A♭	A♭	D♭	E♭
E	E	A	B	D♭	D♭	G♭	A♭
B	B	E	F♯	G♭	G♭	C♭	D♭
F♯	F♯	B	C♯				

PROGRESSIVE BEGINNER BLUES HARMONICA
FOR BEGINNING BLUES HARMONICA PLAYERS
An informative, easy to follow introduction to the world of Blues Harmonica. Introduces cross harp playing immediately and covers essential techniques such as note bending, vibrato, slides, train rhythms, call and response and improvisation.

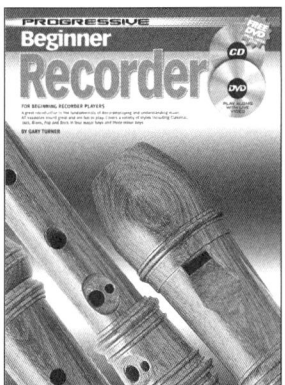

PROGRESSIVE BEGINNER RECORDER
FOR BEGINNING RECORDER PLAYERS
A great introduction to the fundamentals of Recorder playing and understanding music. All examples sound great and are fun to play. Covers a variety of styles including Classical, Jazz, Blues, Pop and Rock in four major keys and three minor keys.

PROGRESSIVE BEGINNER TRUMPET
FOR BEGINNING TRUMPET PLAYERS
A great introduction to the fundamentals of Trumpet playing and understanding music. All examples sound great and are fun to play. Covers a variety of styles including Rock, Jazz, Pop, Classical, and Blues, along with an introduction to improvising.

PROGRESSIVE BEGINNER FLUTE
FOR BEGINNING FLUTE PLAYERS
A great introduction to the fundamentals of Flute playing and understanding music. All examples sound great and are fun to play. Covers a variety of styles including Classical, Jazz, Blues, Pop and Rock, along with an introduction to improvising.

PROGRESSIVE BEGINNER SAXOPHONE
FOR BEGINNING SAXOPHONISTS
A great introduction to the fundamentals of Saxophone playing and understanding music. All examples sound great and are fun to play. Covers a variety of styles including Rock, Jazz, Blues, Pop and Classical, along with an introduction to improvising.

PROGRESSIVE ROCK SAXOPHONE METHOD
FOR BEGINNER TO ADVANCED STUDENTS

Specifically designed for students wishing to play Rock sax, either in a group or solo for fun. The emphasis is on making music immediately. Covers a variety of sounds, rhythms and techniques essential to Rock playing. Also contains lessons on transposing, playing in all keys and improvisation. Anyone who completes this book will be well on the way to becoming an excellent Rock sax player.

PROGRESSIVE BEGINNER ELECTRONIC KEYBOARD
FOR BEGINNER KEYBOARD PLAYERS

An easy to follow Electronic Keyboard method for the complete beginner. Covers note reading, finger technique, using the automatic accompaniment function and playing chords with the left hand. Includes many well known songs in a variety of styles.

PROGRESSIVE BEGINNER PIANO
FOR BEGINNER PIANISTS

An easy to follow Piano method for the complete beginner. Covers note reading, music fundamentals, finger technique and playing chords with the left hand. Includes many well known songs in a variety of styles.

PROGRESSIVE BEGINNER GUITAR
FOR BEGINNER GUITAR STUDENTS

An easy to follow Guitar method for the complete beginner. Covers both melody and chord playing using standard notation and tablature. Introduces all the essential techniques and music fundamentals. Includes chords and melodies of many well known songs in a variety of musical styles.

PROGRESSIVE SLIDE GUITAR TECHNIQUE
FOR BEGINNER TO ADVANCED

A comprehensive, easy to follow guide, introducing all the important techniques required to play Slide Guitar. Including damping, fretting, sliding, vibrato, slide scales and open tunings. Contains over 50 Slide exercises and Solos.

HARMONICA CHART *FOR BEGINNERS*

Notes on the C Harmonica

	1	2	3	4	5	6	7	8	9	10
Exhale	C	E	G	C	E	G	C	E	G	C
Inhale	D	G	B	D	F	A	B	D	F	A
Bend	D♭	F	B♭ or A	D♭	E	A♭				

TABLE OF KEYS & KEY SIGNATURES

Key of C Major
No Sharps or Flats

The most common chords found in the key of C Major are:

C	Dm	Em	F	G^7	Am
Cmaj^7	Dm^7	Em^7	Fmaj^7	G^9	Am^7

Key of G Major
1 Sharp F$\sharp$

The most common chords found in the key of G Major are:

G	Am	Bm	C	D^7	Em
Gmaj^7	Am^7	Bm^7	Cmaj^7	D^9	Em^7

Key of D Major
2 Sharps F$\sharp$, C$\sharp$

The most common chords found in the key of D Major are:

D	Em	F$\sharp$m	G	A^7	Bm
Dmaj^7	Em^7	F$\sharp$m^7	Gmaj^7	A^9	Bm^7

Key of A Major
3 Sharps F$\sharp$, C$\sharp$, G$\sharp$

The most common chords found in the key of A Major are:

A	Bm	C$\sharp$m	D	E^7	F$\sharp$m
Amaj^7	Bm^7	C$\sharp$m^7	Dmaj^7	E^9	F$\sharp$m^7

Key of E Major
4 Sharps F$\sharp$, C$\sharp$, G$\sharp$, D$\sharp$

The most common chords found in the key of E Major are:

E	F$\sharp$m	G$\sharp$m	A	B^7	C$\sharp$m
Emaj^7	F$\sharp$m^7	G$\sharp$m^7	Amaj^7	B^9	C$\sharp$m^7

Key of B Major
5 Sharps F$\sharp$, C$\sharp$, G$\sharp$, D$\sharp$, A$\sharp$

The most common chords found in the key of

HOW TO USE THIS CHART

Note Values

	Whole Note and Rest (Semibreve)	Half Note and Rest (Minim)	Quarter Note and Rest (Crotchet)	Eighth Note and Rest (Quaver)	Sixteenth Note and Rest (Semiquaver)
Quarter note Beat(s):	4	2	1	1/2	1/4

Keys

Always inquire as to what key the song to be played will be in. Sometimes, in informal playing situations, you may have some control over what key to play in. Blues songs will generally be most easily played in second or cross position. So if you can request a key, make certain that it is a key that you can play in cross position. With your C harmonica, this will mean requesting a Blues in G.

TWELVE BAR BLUES

The standard Blues structure is the twelve bar chord structure that is featured throughout the book *Progressive Beginner Harmonica*. It is often worth making sure before beginning a song that this is the chord structure you will be using. Simply asking, "Will we be playing a Twelve Bar Blues?" should be enough to let you know what you will be in for. If the other musicians are not used to playing Blues, they may ask you what chords to use in a Twelve Bar Blues. The chart below will let you describe the chords to use in any key Blues, and the paragragh tells you how to choose what key Blues to play. If they are asking you what chords to use, that usually gives you the right to choose the key. Choose a key from the left-hand column. Reading that row from left to right will tell you which chords to use, and the top row will tell you how many bars to hold each chord for. For convenience, the turnaround is assumed to be a full bar long. You may want to look at the G row, and compare it to the key of G Twelve Bar Blues used in the book *Progressive Beginner Harmonica*. Also many guitarists or keyboard players may sometimes wish to use a chord variation called a seventh chord, which can be subsituted for any of the chords listed below without damaging the structure.

Twelver Bar Blues in Every Key

Key	4 bars	2 bars	2 bars	1 bar	1 bar	1 bar	1 bar
C	C	F	C	G	F	C	G
D$\flat$	D$\flat$	G$\flat$	D$\flat$	A$\flat$	G$\flat$	D$\flat$	A$\flat$
D	D	G	D	A	G	D	A
E$\flat$	E$\flat$	A$\flat$	E$\flat$	B$\flat$	A$\flat$	E$\flat$	B$\flat$
E	E	A	E	B	A	E	B

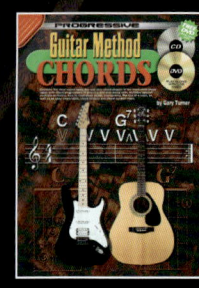

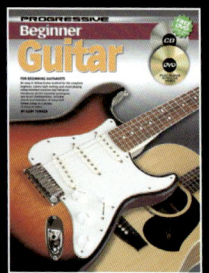

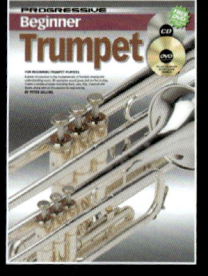
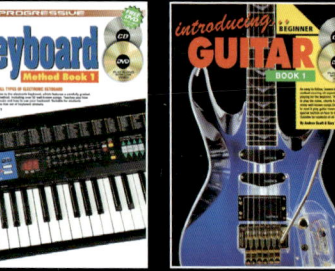
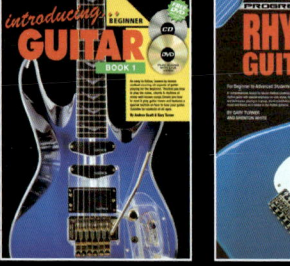
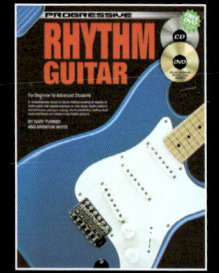

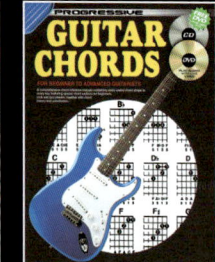
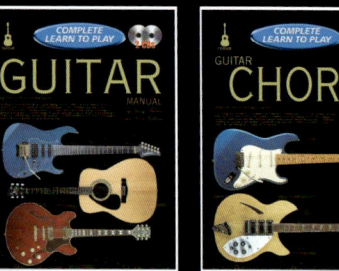

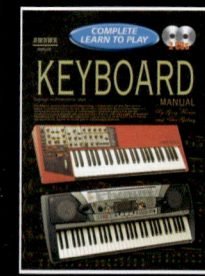
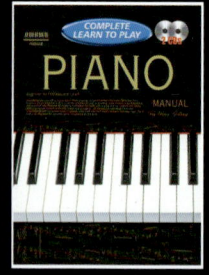

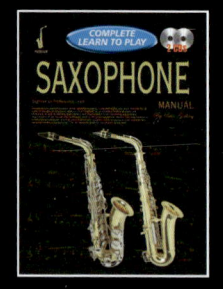
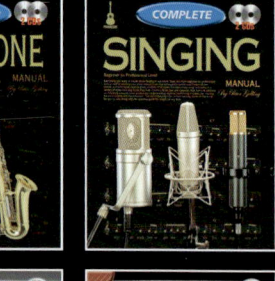
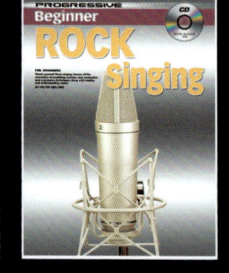

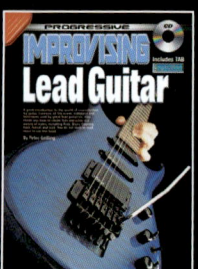
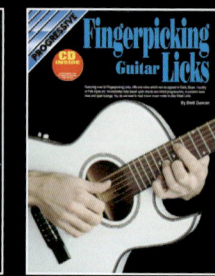
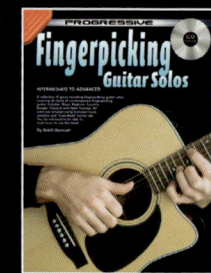

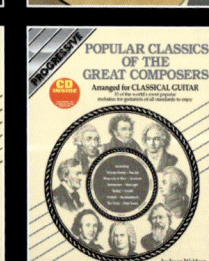
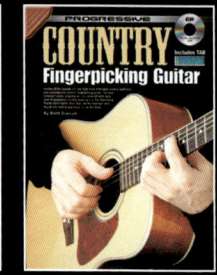

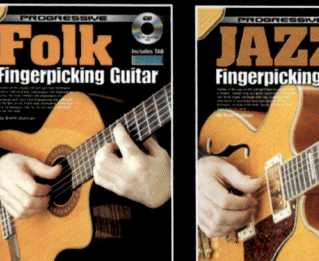
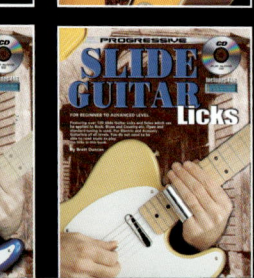

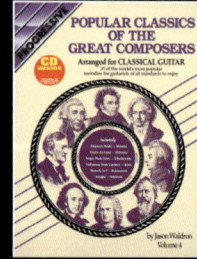
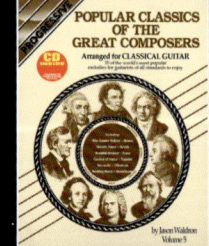
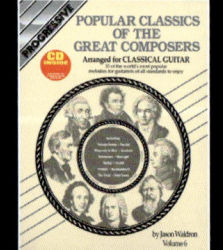

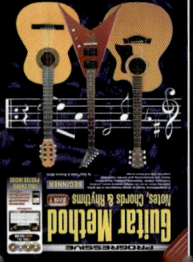
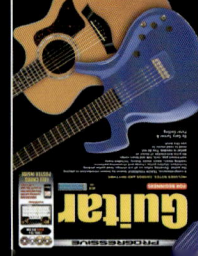

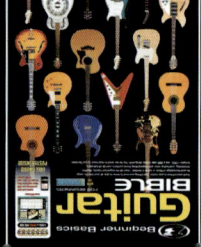

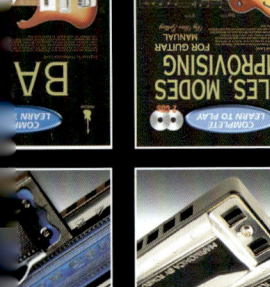

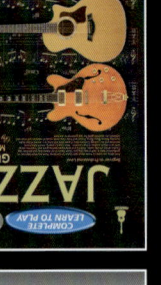

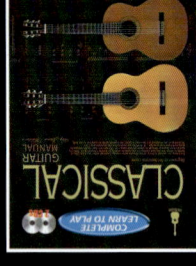
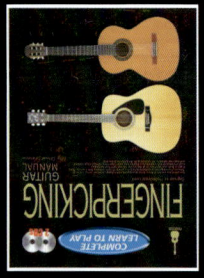
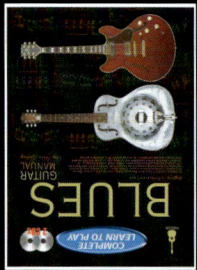
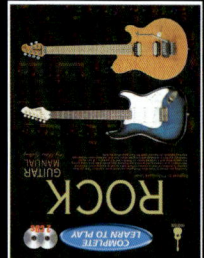
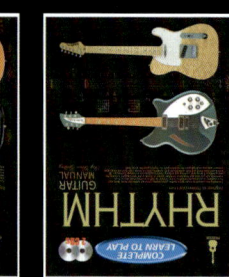
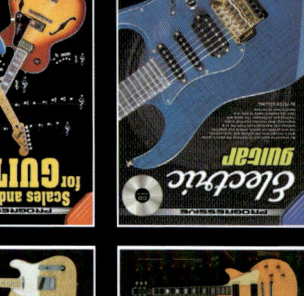

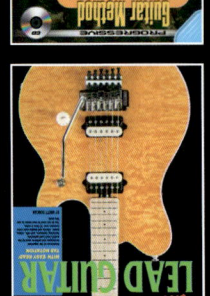
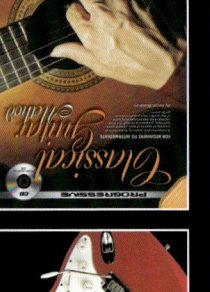

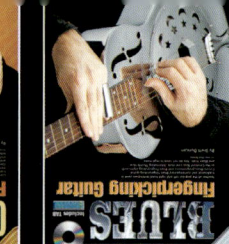
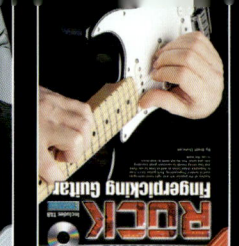

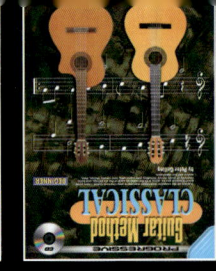
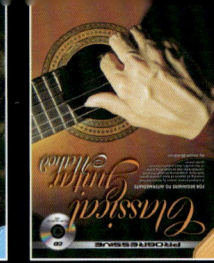

Holding the harmonica

Mouthing the harmonica

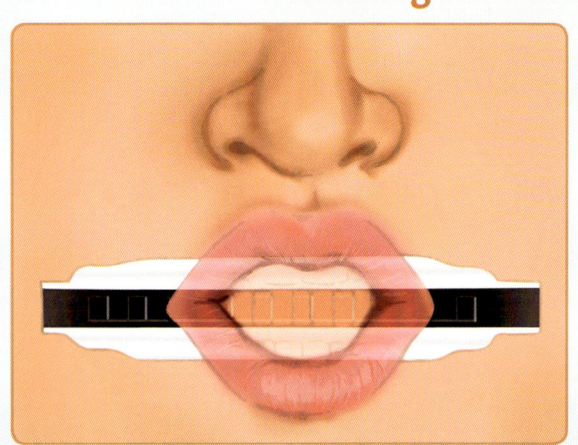

Tongu

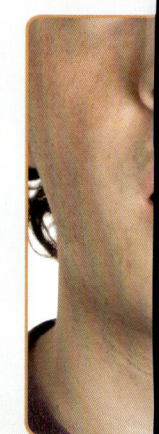

Hand Vibrato

Puck

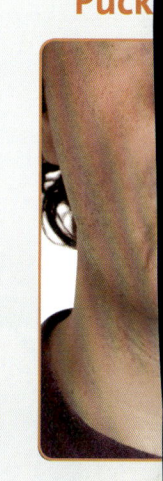

Bmaj⁷ C#m⁷ D#m⁷ Emaj⁷ F#⁹ G#m⁷

Key of F# Major
6 Sharps
F#, C#, G#
D#, A#, E#

The most common chords found in the key of F# Major are:

F#	G#m	A#m	B	C#⁷	D#m
F#maj⁷	G#m⁷	A#m⁷	Bmaj⁷	C#⁹	D#m⁷

Key of F Major
1 Flat
B♭

The most common chords found in the key of F Major are:

F	Gm	Am	B♭	C⁷	Dm
Fmaj⁷	Gm⁷	Am⁷	B♭maj7	C⁹	Dm⁷

Key of B♭ Major
2 Flats
B♭, E♭

The most common chords found in the key of B♭ Major are:

B♭	Cm	Dm	E♭	F⁷	Gm
B♭maj⁷	Cm⁷	Dm⁷	E♭maj⁷	F⁹	Gm⁷

Key of E♭ Major
3 Flats
B♭, E♭, A♭

The most common chords found in the key of E♭ Major are:

E♭	Fm	Gm	A♭	B♭⁷	Cm
E♭maj⁷	Fm⁷	Gm⁷	A♭maj⁷	B♭⁹	Cm⁷

Key of A♭ Major
4 Flats
B♭, E♭, A♭
D♭

The most common chords found in the key of A♭ Major are:

A♭	B♭m	Cm	D♭	E♭⁷	Fm
A♭maj⁷	B♭m⁷	Cm⁷	D♭maj⁷	E♭⁹	Fm⁷

Key of D♭ Major
5 Flats
B♭, E♭, A♭
D♭, G♭

The most common chords found in the key of D♭ Major are:

D♭	E♭m	Fm	G♭	A♭⁷	B♭m
D♭maj⁷	E♭m⁷	Fm⁷	G♭maj⁷	A♭⁹	B♭m⁷

Blocking

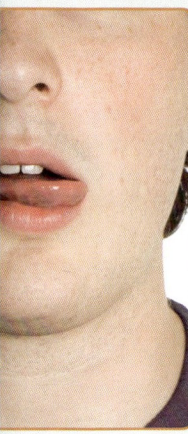

Method / **er Method**

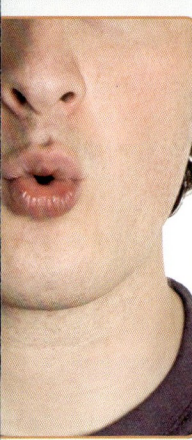

G	G	C	G	D	C	G	D
A♭	A♭	D♭	A♭	E♭	D♭	A♭	E♭
A	A	D	A	E	D	A	E
B♭	B♭	E♭	B♭	F	E♭	B♭	F
B	B	E	B	F#	E	B	F#

CROSS HARP PLAYING

The following chart lists all the keys used in music along with the correct harmonica for playing second position cross harp in each key. The easiest way to check if you are using the right harmonica for the key is to play holes ② (inhale), or **3**, or **6** (exhale) and see if it is the same note as the key you want by testing it against a guitar or keyboard chord. If the guitar plays a **D chord**, your note should be a **D note**, if the guitar plays an **F chord**, your note should be an F note, etc. You can usually tell by ear if you have the correct note or not.

Second Position Chart

Guitar Key	Harmonica Key
C	F
G	C
D	G
A	D
E	A
B	E
F#	B
D	G♭
A♭	D♭
E♭	A♭
B♭	E♭
F	B♭

oPlayMusic™

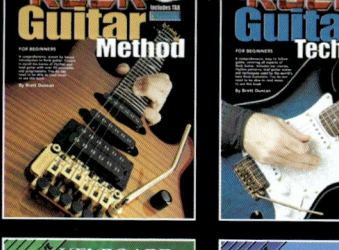
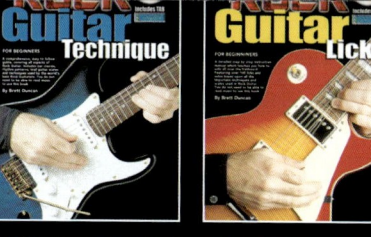
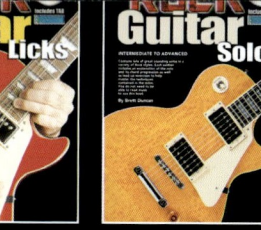
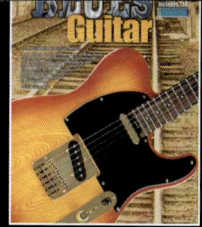
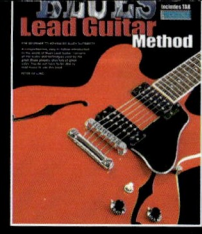
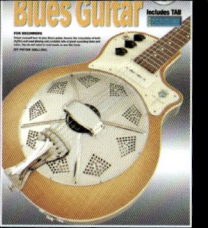
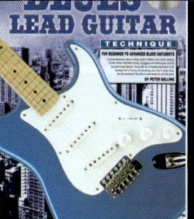

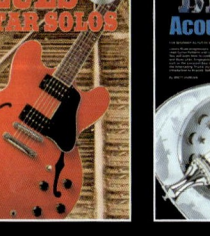

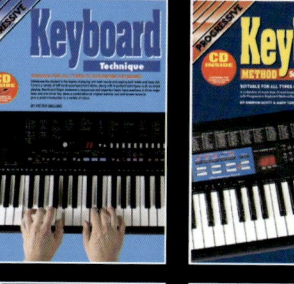
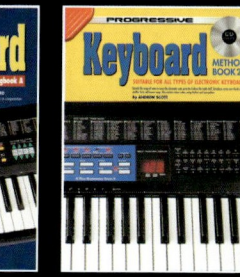
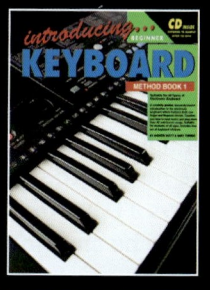
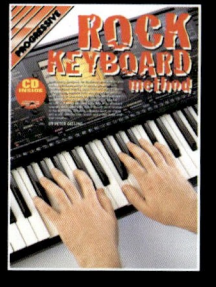
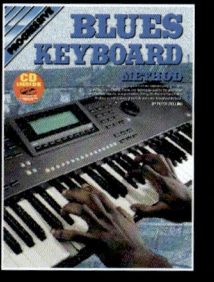

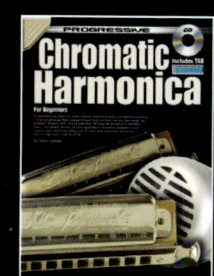
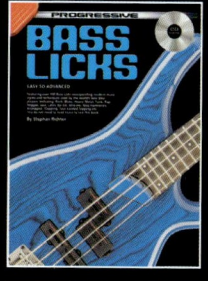

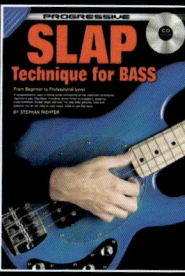

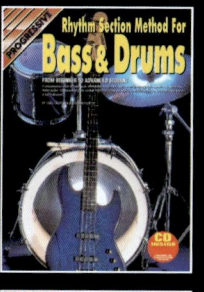
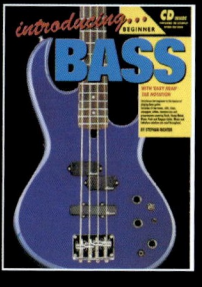

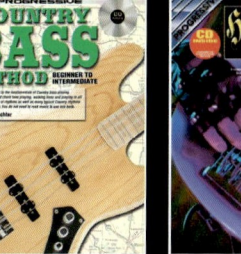

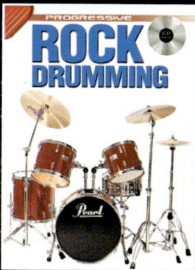

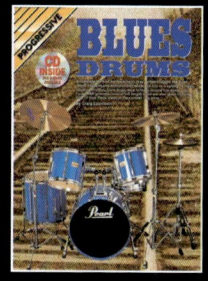

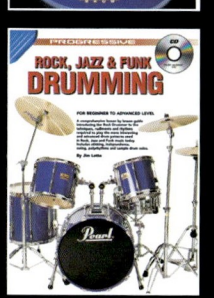
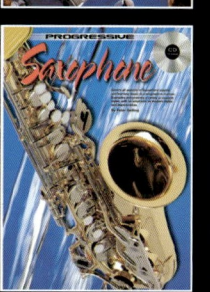
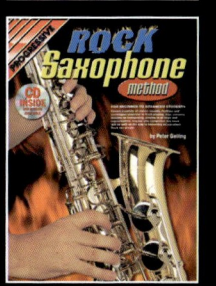

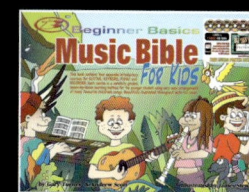
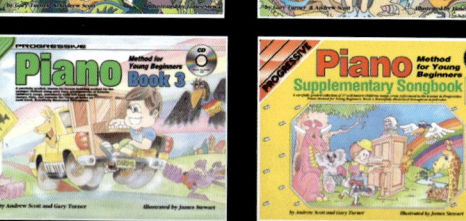
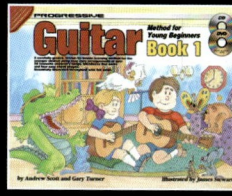
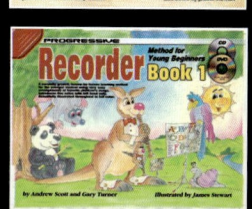

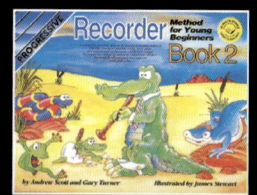
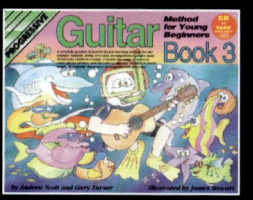
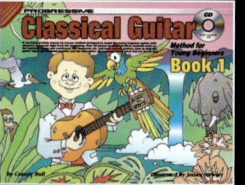
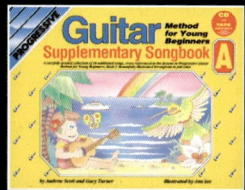

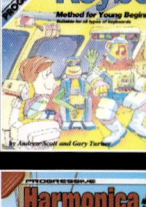